PETER SHAFFER

STEIN AND DAY/*Publishers*/New York

Designed by Bernard Schleifer

Printed in the United States of America

Stein and Day/*Publishers*/7 East 48 Street, New York, N.Y. 10017

Photographs by courtesy of Friedman-Abeles

BY THE SAME AUTHOR

Five Finger Exercise

The Private Ear: The Public Eye

The Royal Hunt of the Sun

WHITE LIES   *Page 5*

BLACK COMEDY   *Page 43*

Black Comedy was first presented at Chichester, England by the National Theatre on July 27, 1965, and subsequently at The Old Vic Theatre, London, with the following cast:

BRINDSLEY MILLER	Derek Jacobi
CAROL MELKETT	Louise Purnell
MISS FURNIVAL	Doris Hare
COLONEL MELKETT	Graham Crowden
HAROLD GORRINGE	Albert Finney
SCHUPPANZIGH	Paul Curran
CLEA	Maggie Smith
GEORG BAMBERGER	Michael Byrne

Black Comedy and *White Lies* were first presented in New York at the Ethel Barrymore Theater on February 12, 1967 by Alexander Cohen with the following cast:

WHITE LIES

SOPHIE: BARONESS LEMBERG	Geraldine Page
FRANK	Donald Madden
TOM	Michael Crawford

BLACK COMEDY

BRINDSLEY MILLER	Michael Crawford
CAROL MELKETT	Lynn Redgrave
MISS FURNIVAL	Camila Ashland
COLONEL MELKETT	Peter Bull
HAROLD GORRINGE	Donald Madden
SCHUPPANZIGH	Pierre Epstein
CLEA	Geraldine Page
GEORG BAMBERGER	Michael Miller

All three productions were directed by JOHN DEXTER.

WHITE
LIES

For
Paul
with
love

Characters

SOPHIE: BARONESS LEMBERG

FRANK

TOM

PLACE: *The play happens in the Fortune Teller's parlor of* SOPHIE, BARONESS LEMBERG, *on the promenade of a run-down seaside resort on the south coast of England.*

TIME: *The present. Around six o'clock in the evening: mid-September.*

SOPHIE's *Parlor is in fact a seedy living room facing the sea. One side of it is almost entirely occupied by a window, in which is spelled out in cheap gold letters (and in reverse, so that it can be read from outside):* BARONESS LEMBERG, PALMISTE. CLAIRVOYANTE. *And in smaller letters:* CONSULTANT TO ROYALTY. *Through this window you can glimpse a rusting iron balustrade, painted resort-green, and the bleak six o'clock sky of a disastrous English September.*

The entrance is on the other side, and leads into a sort of waiting room, partially visible when the door is open. A second door takes you from the waiting room into the streets; over it is suspended a loud bell to warn SOPHIE *if* SHE *has a client.*

The room is occupied by dusty, broken-down furniture. The most noticeable article of this is the fortune-telling table: an old chilblained Victorian thing, covered with baize and placed centrally on a rotting carpet. On either side of it stands an equally bunioned Victorian chair—and the same swollen decrepitude extends to the sideboard at the right and the little dressing table at the back.

There are two photographs in the room. One, on a wall, is of a huge man's hand and is clearly visible. The other—larger, and far more important to the action—stands on the side table with its back to the audience and, save for the frame, is in-

visible. This is a picture of Vassili, SOPHIE's *friend. It stands as far as possible from the other important friend in her life: Pericles the Parakeet—who is equally invisible inside his wire cage by the window. The* BARONESS' *life in this room alternates between these two poles, the photograph and the cage.*

As the curtain rises, the stage is apparently empty. Presently, however, we hear the sound of singing, issuing from one of the high-backed Victorian chairs facing directly upstage: "A Hard Day's Night" sung in a Germanic accent. Presently a hand lifts up and throws a whole fan of playing cards irritatedly onto the table. SOPHIE *has evidently been playing patience.* SHE *rises wearily and moves over to the window, through which the light comes drear and thick.*

SOPHIE *is a woman of about forty-eight years old. Her appearance is rather neglected; bears the palpable signs of poverty; and is not enhanced by a German fondness for blouses and long woolen skirts. When* SHE *speaks her voice is marked by a marked, but never incomprehensible, German accent, and her delivery is mainly swift and vigorous.*

Now SHE *stares through the window in bleak distress.*

SOPHIE. Look at it. The sea. Like they've poured out ten million cups of tea. No wonder they call it the English Channel. Not one gleam of sunlight in ten days! Not one soul out. Not one miserable holidaymaker walking, jetty to jetty. Nothing but wet sand, rusty iron—and salt on the windows . . . Grinmouth-on-Sea: Fairyland of the South coast! Grinmouth-on-Tea! (*To the photo.*) You hear that, Vassi, I made a joke. (*Sarcastic.*) Oh no, don't laugh. The Germans have no sense of humor, it's well known. Only the Greeks are witty, jaja, I'm sure . . . (*To the cage.*) Perry likes it anyway, don't you? No? . . . Are you sulking too? Well, I

don't blame you. Poor little Pericles. Look, I'll tell your fortune—cheer you up? . . . Ja? . . . "You are to fly away on a
long long journey!" (SHE *laughs*.) . . . Only where would you
go, poor little thing? Down the promenade to the chemist?
Up to the Fish and Chips Shop? . . . One thing is sure,
you'd never find your way home again.

(*Gulls and wind.*)

Beloved God, this silence! You would think someone would
consult me, if only to ask should they kill themselves! . . .
Do you know what I think? Everybody has left town behind
our backs. Just taken a train—the whole population at once,
away to London—and we are left: Sophie—Vassili—and Pericles the Parakeet. The unholy three! . . . Do you realize
there hasn't been an actual human being in this place for
six days? And then it was only Mr. Bowler Hat—if you call
him human! "Mrs. Lemberg, I have to inform you you owe a
million pounds in rent!" Or was it two? Next time he comes
he'll close us: that's for certain. I haven't paid him a penny
since June. (*Irritated.*) Oh, Vassili, what's funny *now*? Do
you never do anything but giggle? Honest, sometimes I don't
understand you at all. Maybe it's specially Greek to laugh
at the serious things of life: if so, I don't appreciate it! I'm
in real difficulties, don't you understand? I owe two months'
rent, and not a client for days. Is that so amusing? . . .
Sometimes I think you're going to stay a child all your life . . .

(SHE *walks away from the photograph, then stops.*)

What's that? . . . How charming! What an exquisite thing
to say! I suppose you think you're talking to one of your
upstart ladies from Athens. Well, let me remind you who I
am. A Lemberg. The Baroness Lemberg. (*Sharply.*) You came
here to learn history, well, so—here's some homework for
you. My family was great under Maria Theresa. What you

had then in your so wonderful Greece were goats. Human goats, my dear, living on curd milk! All right? . . . (*Exasperated.*) Oh for God's sake now, are you going to sulk? All right—join Perry. Sulks for the evening: how amusing! . . . I spend my life with a bird and a child, and I don't know which is the more boring!

(SHE *sits. Her tone becomes penitent.*)

I'm sorry, Vassi: my tongue runs off with me sometimes. I know how dreary it is for you in the house. Go out and see Irina. I tell you what: why don't you invite her here tomorrow for tea? . . . (*Sweetly.*) Ja, of course I mean it! You are charming together—I like to see you with her, I've told you. You are so perfect together. So right together. Really. Right together . . .

(*The bell clashes.* SOPHIE *is startled.*)

Who is it?

(*Silence.*)

Who is it?

(*Silence.*

Speaking through the crack.)

One minute, please. Would you mind waiting in the room down the corridor? I'll receive you in a moment! . . .

(*Shutting the door.*)

Beloved God, there are two of them! Two whole clients! I don't believe it. And on a day like this—it's incredible! . . . That's two whole pounds—think of it. Four if they take the crystal ball.

(SHE *adjusts her hair, takes her shawl and fan.*)

Well they're going to take the crystal ball whether they like it or not . . . I only hope I can remember everything. One gets so rusty! . . . (*To Vassili.*) Oh shut up, you!—that's not funny . . . Ja, I have news for you. It takes a fraud to

call a fraud: that's what I say! You were a liar in your baby
carriage, I'm sure of it! . . . (*Addressing herself to the
plants.*) Oh don't droop so—boring middle class plant! . . .
Now come on everyone, for God's sake! A little regality
around here, please!

(SHE *opens the door.*)

I'm ready now. Come in please, one of you!

(FRANK *enters: a boy of about twenty-five, cold, watchful,
ambiguous.* HE *wears a leather jacket.* SOPHIE *is immediately
alarmed.*)

FRANK. Are you the witch?

SOPHIE. I am the Baroness Lemberg.

FRANK. Consultant to royalty?

SOPHIE. Exactly.

FRANK. You mean thrones have tottered at the flick of your
ace-king-jack?

SOPHIE. Perhaps.

(HE *lounges across the room and looks at the photograph
on the wall.*)

FRANK. Whose hand is that?

SOPHIE. A murderer. That is the left hand of Ulf Momsen, the
Stockholm Strangler. It has the most remarkable Line of
Fate. You can see the suicide in it, quite clearly.

FRANK. You *can?*

SOPHIE. *I* can.

FRANK. I like your slogan outside: "Lemberg Never Lies." Is it
true?

SOPHIE. Of course.

FRANK. What a pity.

SOPHIE. I beg your pardon?

FRANK. This place stinks a bit, doesn't it? Bird shit and tinned

[13]

spaghetti. I suppose you eat it to improve your mystic powers.
(*Examining the cage.*) Who's this? Your familiar?

SOPHIE. Please?

FRANK. All witches have familiars, don't they? Creepy little animals they share confidences with. I suppose you'd lose all
your mystic powers without him, wouldn't you? (*To the
bird.*) Hallo, then. What's up with you? Miserable little bugger aren't you? . . . I bet you've heard some nasty predic-
tions in this room, eh?

SOPHIE. Stand away, mister, please. He's a very sensitive bird.

FRANK. That's all right. I'm an expert on sensitive birds.

SOPHIE. (*Sharply.*) I told you, he's sensitive. So please come
away from there!

FRANK. What a harsh lady.

SOPHIE. I imagine you want your fortune told. Let me give you
my scale of charges. (SHE *hands him a board.*) One pound for
cards alone. Thirty shillings for cards and palms. Two pounds
for the crystal ball. The ball of course is by far the most profound. It costs just a little more—but then in this world, if
one wants the best, one has to pay for it, doesn't one?
(SHE *gives him a ravishing smile.*)

FRANK. Yes.

SOPHIE. So which will it be?

FRANK. None.

SOPHIE. I beg your pardon?

FRANK. None.

SOPHIE. Then . . . what do you want?

FRANK. A giggle.

SOPHIE. A giggle?

FRANK. Yeh. We live in dull times. It's our duty to make them
gayer, don't you agree? I hope you like jokes yourself.

SOPHIE. If the situation is amusing, sir, I think I can manage a
—what? A giggle . . .

FRANK. Good. A humorous lady! I'm glad to hear that, Baroness. Because that's what I want to consult you about. That's
what I want to create right here in this room—an amusing
situation.

SOPHIE. Create?

FRANK. Exactly. For him—the boy who's come here with me.
You see, him and me, we have this crazy relationship going,
like, well we kid all the time—have the laugh on each other:
you know. What they call practical jokes. Some people think
it's adolescent. I hope you don't.

SOPHIE. That depends.

FRANK. He's a clever kid—very impressionable. I got him here
to see you by telling him you were one of the most famous
fortune tellers in the western world. Doing a summer season
for her health's sake.

(SHE *lowers her eyes and makes modest noises.*)

His name's Tom, and he's lead singer with our group. We're
called the White Lies. I don't suppose you've ever heard of
us.

SOPHIE. On the contrary, you are singing tonight: . . . (*in the
manner of a clairvoyante*) at the Holiday Camp!

FRANK. (*Impressed.*) How d'you know that?

SOPHIE. (*Laughing.*) I saw it on the poster! You're on the same
bill with the Lettuce Leaves. That's a pity: they're lousy.
However, you have the Serial Numbers to top the bill, and
they are excellent.

FRANK. Well, well, a fan!

SOPHIE. A vulgar word, but true. Are you any good?

FRANK. He's good. A real talent. The girls go mad for him . . .

SOPHIE. And you? Do you sing also?

FRANK. Me? No. I'm their Manager.

SOPHIE. Well!

FRANK. (*Staring at her.*) That's my scene, really. I manage.

SOPHIE. (*Nervous.*) How interesting.

FRANK. It can be. It's why I'm here now—to manage this little scene . . . (HE *smiles at her again.*) When we drove into Grinmouth this afternoon and I saw your sign, I thought to myself immediately: Baroness Lemberg, you're the lady for me. In your mysterious parlor I could stage the best joke ever played. I could get him so brilliantly he'd never forget it.

SOPHIE. (*Coldly.*) Really?

FRANK. With your help, of course. And with someone of your fame—consultant to royalty and all that—I wouldn't expect you to do it for nothing. I'm prepared to offer quite a large fee. I'll do anything for a giggle. I really will. (HE *gives his smile.*)

SOPHIE. (*Interested despite herself.*) What kind of giggle would this be exactly, mister?

FRANK. Well it's sort of a game, really. I'd want you to tell him his past, present, and future.

SOPHIE. Well, that's my profession, after all.

FRANK. I mean precisely. I don't mean to be rude—I'm sure you're fine on your own—but with me you'd be perfect, you see? In this envelope are the main facts of Tom's life—things he's told me over the past year. No one else knows them but me. Some of it's pretty lurid stuff. Unhappy childhood. Coal-mining background. Drunken father who beat him and threw his guitar on the fire. It's all here.

SOPHIE. And are you suggesting I *use* this?

FRANK. Well now listen. Tom's a bit dim but he's not an idiot.

You'll have your work cut out for you to convince him you're genuine. That's where the fun comes in. By the time you've finished telling back to him what's in here, he'll be fish-mouthed.

SOPHIE. Mister, I see no joke in this. It's not funny at all.

(*Pause.*)

FRANK. To be honest, Baroness, this game isn't entirely for laughs. Mainly, but not entirely. I see it as a sort of warning game. Like I'm using it to say something to him. Do you understand? I mean, if you can get Tom to the point when he really believes you have the power to see his whole life, he'll really believe you when you see something a bit nasty in his future. It'll sort of scare him off a bit. Do you see?

SOPHIE. Scare him off what?

FRANK. A girl. I told you I was interested in sensitive birds. (*Staring at her necklace, which* SHE *is fingering.*) What are *they*?

SOPHIE. Greek worry beads.

FRANK. Are you worried?

SOPHIE. Why should I be?

FRANK. Her name's Helen, and she's the girl in our Group. She's got a nice voice—nothing special, but it can carry a tune and won't sour the cream. I've known her for a couple of years, on and off. Mostly *on*, if you follow me. In fact these last eighteen months we've had what I'd call a perfect working relationship.

SOPHIE. It sounds very romantic.

FRANK. (*Lightly.*) It isn't romantic: it works, or did till he came along. Tom the Talent. Then things began to change. Mostly with her. She found she couldn't resist all that shy working class charm. The downcast look—Yorkshire mur-

mur: very trendy . . . And when she looked—he looked. I
don't exactly know what's been going on between them:
nothing much I should think at the moment. She's too timid
and he's too hung up on his loyalty to me, which he damn
well should be by the way. I gave that boy a marvelous bloody
chance. And this is his way of repaying me. He thinks I don't
know, you know. Well, it's time we undeceived him, isn't it.

SOPHIE. You are in love with this girl?

FRANK. That word's rather got rigor mortis round the edges,
hasn't it? (HE *laughs.*) Look: the way we are is the way I like
it. Cool . . . easy . . . nothing strenuous . . . Anyway, if
there's any leaving ever done in my life I do it: do you see?
. . . (*Quietly.*) Can't you leave them alone?

(SHE *stops fiddling with the beads.*
HE *smiles.*)

I suppose that's why they're called worry beads. Because they
worry other people.

(SHE *returns his smile even more uncertainly. A pause.*)

Well, let's get back to my little game, shall we? By this time
you've done his past and present, and as far as he's concerned you're the hottest thing since the Witch of Endor.
Right. Now you move in for the grand finale. I want you to
have a vision, Baroness. A strange, symbolic vision. Let's set
it right . . . (*Slowly.*) You look a little deeper into your
crystal ball and you see pink. Shocking pink. Helen's dressing
gown. Yeh, that's a good touch—very intimate. You see her
wearing it, a pretty blonde girl lying on a bed. Describe the
bed. Brass rails top and bottom, and above it, a picture on
the wall: some droopy tart holding a lily and flopping her
tresses over a stone balcony. It's called Art Nouveau, which
is French for Sentimental Rubbish. Helen loves it of course!
Anyway, use it. Establish the room. *My* room. You'll have

him goggling! Now look deeper. "Good heavens, there's someone else on the bed! Why, it's you, Tom! And what are you doing, my dear? Gracious me, what a passionate creature you are! You're kissing her neck, running your fingers through her blonde hair . . . (*Mockingly.*) Inside that thin frame of yours is a raging animal, isn't there? . . ." (HE *laughs.*) I'd love to be here during that bit. They've never even held hands I shouldn't think.

SOPHIE. Go on, please.

FRANK. (*Carefully.*) Well now you'll have to darken it a bit, won't you? . . . Change the mood. I'd thought of something like this. I hope you like it . . . The door opens. A man stands there. You can't see his face but he's wearing a green corduroy jacket, with black piping round the lapels. That'll get him best, a detail like that. The lovers look up, eyes wide and guilty! Corduroy begins to move towards them. They try to rise, but they're like glued on the bed. Slow motion. Him coming on—them tangled in the sheets—trying to escape. He arrives at the foot of the bed and suddenly—his hand shoots out—like an order!—and what? Why, the girl's whole manner alters at once. She smiles—takes the hand—allows herself to be lifted up, light as a pink feather—high over the brass rails to safety. Our Tom is left alone . . . And now you see scare in the ball! Tom staring at them both. Them staring back, laughing. Yeh. And what's that now in her hands? Something—it looks like a metal can. Yes, a large metal can. She raises it—upends it—begins to pour from it over the sheets. And then, slowly, Corduroy raises his hands too—a matchbox in the air—strikes it—drops a match on to the bed. (*Very quietly.*) Oh look, the orange! Soft fire like orange squirrels running over the bed, over his legs, over his arms, up on to his head . . . his head bursts into flowers! (*Gesturing dream-*

ily.) The whole ball becomes orange—flame whirling, raging inside the crystal, obliterating everything. Then slowly it sinks in. Glass pales from orange to pink, to grey: it clears. And then you see him. Tom the Talent. Still sitting upright on my bed—mouth open, one arm raised—like a salute to death. The only difference is—the whole figure is made of ash. (*Pause.*) Interpret that vision, Baroness. Question it. "Who is this corduroy jacket?" "That's Frank" he'll say. "Well know something, Tom. Frank and that girl are right together. Leave them alone."

SOPHIE. (*Softly.*) "Right together?"

FRANK. "If you come between them, it'll mean disaster for you. Maybe even death."

SOPHIE. "Right together."

FRANK. "Right together." "Belong together." What's it matter? Just so long as you scare him out of his wits.

SOPHIE. For a giggle.

FRANK. Yes, a joke, that's it. We all of us have different senses of humor, Baroness.

SOPHIE. Who am I?

FRANK. What's that?

SOPHIE. Who am I? Some silly gypsy bitch in a caravan you can buy for a couple of pounds?

FRANK. I was thinking of more than that.

SOPHIE. (*Angry.*) Four—five—what's the difference? It's what you think, I can see it: the mad old fake, she'll take anything I offer. Well, mister, let me tell you: you're dealing with a very different kind of lady, I assure you!

FRANK. Oh, come off it!

SOPHIE. (SHE *thrusts her hand at him.*) Look at this! It has held the hand of a Grand Duchess in intimate spiritual communion! It has held Governors—Ministers of Justice—Princes of the Blood!

FRANK. Yes, I see them now—thronging the outer salon!

SOPHIE. Very amusing. Look, mister, I'm not mad, you know, there are no Duchesses out there, I know that. Just crazy spinsters, stinking of moth balls, old red men with gin in their eyes, begging me to predict just one horse race, one football pool, to make them rich for life. Rubbish people, all of them, boring me to death with their second-rate dreams. Nevertheless, I make adjustment. Other years—other tears! I spend my life now casting prophetic pearls before middle class swine. But one thing always: I may hate them, but I do not cheat them. *Lemberg never lies!*
(*Pause.*)

FRANK. (*Quietly.*) Is that how you think of me, Baroness? One of the swine?

SOPHIE. (*Frightened.*) Of course not.

FRANK. I hope not. I really do hope not.

SOPHIE. I merely say . . .

FRANK. (*Interested.*) What do you merely say?

SOPHIE. That if you think I betray my art for a few pounds, you are badly mistaken.

FRANK. Would I be equally mistaken if it was twenty-five pounds?

SOPHIE. Twenty-five?

FRANK. As you said, if you want the best, you've got to pay for it.

SOPHIE. I don't understand. Why don't you just tell him to leave her alone?

FRANK. If I do anything, Baroness, I do it with style. My own style. You do your job right, this'll work a treat.

SOPHIE. He may guess.

FRANK. And even if he does—he'll still get the message. What's

your answer? . . . Look—we've kept him waiting long
enough. Yes or no?

SOPHIE. Disgusting! It's disgusting! . . .

FRANK. Twenty-five quid, dear.

(*Pause.*)

SOPHIE. (*Low.*) All right!

FRANK. A sensible lady. I'll go and fetch him.

SOPHIE. (*Disturbed.*) No—wait!

FRANK. What?

SOPHIE. Give me a minute, please, I must learn this stuff . . .
(SHE *picks up the envelope.*)

FRANK. All right. I'll keep him waiting, tell him how great you
were, reading me. But hurry it up.

SOPHIE. Ja, ja . . . I'll call out when I'm ready.

FRANK. O.K. (HE *goes to the door.*) No tricks now, Baroness.
I would hate you to try keeping that money without earning
it. When he comes out of this room I want to see scare in
his face, like I've never ever seen it.
(HE *goes out.*
SHE *stares after him in horror.*)

SOPHIE. Beloved God! Beloved God, beloved God, beloved God!
. . . (*Shouting at the photo.*) Ja, I know, he's a nut—one
more horror, so what? You've seen them before. The world
is full of perverts. Business is business, for God's sake. And
there's almost half the rent here—just for ten minutes' work!
Anyway, what's it matter? He'll be another horror, just you
see! A little backstreet nothing who wants to be a singer because he can't do a decent day's work! He'll deserve it!
Everyone deserves it! Look, everyone cheats a little, my darling, even your Greek witches. What do you think your famous oracle at Delphi was doing?—one silly cow sitting in a
lot of smoke, saying exactly what she was paid to say! Any-

way I tell you once more and that's the end. It is the duty of the aristocracy to maintain itself, no matter what! Now kindly leave me to study these!

(SHE *sits and writes carefully on her fan.*)

"Born 1945 . . . Coal mines . . . Mother dead. Father drunkard . . . Guitar." Now!

(SHE *tears open the envelope and shows him the money.*) Look! Do you see? I bet you've never seen so much money in all your life! Think what it means! More Beatle records, more little hats like you were starting the Russian Revolution! And next Sunday, if you are good, a taxi—and not a lousy bus! What do you say? . . . All right, go to her! Always the same threat—the same threat. If that's the best you can manage—then go to her. See if I care!

(SHE *rolls the money, snaps a rubber band over it, and thrusts it inside her blouse. Then* SHE *opens the door.*)

Misters!

(*Returning.*)

Go—go—go—go!

(FRANK *returns with* TOM. HE *is a shy-looking boy of twenty-two, with a thick Cheshire accent.* FRANK *is now very calm, and over-polite.*)

FRANK. This is my friend Tom. Tom, this is the Baroness Lemberg. The greatest fortune teller in the world.

SOPHIE. (*Modestly.*) Please! . . . How do you do?

TOM. Hallo.

FRANK. I've been telling him how incredible you are. I hope you don't mind.

SOPHIE. Such powers as I have, mister, I regard as a gift from the Lord God.

FRANK. Just what I was telling him. It's almost a religious experience, being read by you.

SOPHIE. I do my best to convey the truth as I see it.

FRANK. And lady, you certainly see it! I was wondering actually
if I could stay and watch you read him. I'd be very quiet.

SOPHIE. I'm afraid that's quite out of the question. Your emanations would be very disturbing.

FRANK. Couldn't you just ignore my emanations?

SOPHIE. I appreciate your enthusiasm, mister. People of art are
always nourished by enthusiasm. All the same I have a basic
rule. One client: one set of emanations.

TOM. Dead right!

FRANK. Very well.

SOPHIE. May I suggest you go for a promenade? When you re-
turn in fifteen minutes, you will be refreshed and your friend,
I hope, satisfied.

FRANK. Fine. (*To* TOM.) Good luck, then. You're in for a marvelous time, I can tell you. (HE *goes.*)

SOPHIE. So. Sit down, please. (HE *sits.*) Such a flatterer, your
friend.

TOM. No, I think he means it. I've never seen him so excited.
He's not easily impressed, I can tell you.

SOPHIE. Nor you.

TOM. Me?

SOPHIE. You have disbelieving eyes.

TOM. Oh, yeah?

SOPHIE. (*Quickly.*) You will take the crystal ball of course!

TOM. Will I?

SOPHIE. Of course, my dear. It's more profound. And I can see
you deserve the most profound measures.

TOM. Thank you!

SOPHIE. (*Getting the ball.*) You're a musician.

(HE *is startled.*)

Oh don't worry! Remember, I've just read your friend. I presume you are in the Group he manages. It's an easy guess, after all.

(SHE *sets the ball down on the table.*)

There. Just a ball of glass. Except of course that nothing is *just* anything. Give me something you wear, please . . . (HE *starts taking off his overcoat.*) A handkerchief will do. (HE *gives her his handkerchief.*) Thank you. You're very pale. Why?

TOM. No sun, I suppose.

SOPHIE. (*Sitting.*) It's enough, God knows. Every day I look at the sea and hate it all over again. Not once this year have I seen it blue. I think: that's not a sea—it's a gutter between here and France! (SHE *uncovers the ball and puts his handkerchief on it.*) Hang your coat up: you're here for a few minutes, after all.

TOM. (*Rising.*) Thanks.

SOPHIE. All the same I'd say you don't care too much for the sun. You have a winter face.

TOM. Me?

SOPHIE. You like winter best, ja? Rain and storms?

TOM. Could be.

SOPHIE. You're cautious with me. You have no need.

TOM. I'm sorry. Frank said not to say anything at all.

SOPHIE. I think we can discuss the weather without you thinking me a fraud.

TOM. (*Smiling.*) I think so too. You're right. I love days like this. And seaside towns—but only out of season. When no one's there.

SOPHIE. Like here *in* season.

TOM. Oh much worse! I mean, deserted. Dead, dead of winter! . . . I went to Herne Bay last March. It was so cold the rims of your ears felt like they were being gnawed through. The tide was out, and there was snow on the seaweed.

SOPHIE. Snow?

TOM. Yes, it popped when you walked on it. All the sea gulls were sitting in those little shelters that are for people in the summertime. They looked like rows of old convalescents, huddled down in their coat collars.

(SHE *stares at him. Wind, outside the window.*)

SOPHIE. Mister, I do not feel so well this evening. I'm afraid I won't be able to read you.

TOM. You won't?

SOPHIE. I have a headache coming. I feel it. In a minute it will be very painful.

TOM. How do you know?

SOPHIE. (*Loftily.*) Migraine is one of the penalties of divination!

TOM. I'm sorry.

SOPHIE. You'll have to go. You can wait for your friend in the other room.

TOM. Yes. Well . . . good-bye.

SOPHIE. Ja.

(HE *takes his coat and goes to the door.* HE *hesitates.*)

You want something?

TOM. No.

SOPHIE. Er . . . Your handkerchief.

TOM. Oh! Yes!

(HE *comes back to claim it.* SHE *hands it to him.*)

SOPHIE. Can that be only no sun—your paleness?

TOM. What else?

SOPHIE. You think I'm a fake. But somewhere in the back of your head, as you walked here tonight, you were thinking something. Well?

TOM. I suppose what you always think about fortune tellers.

You read stories of people going in for a laugh, coming out changed for life.

SOPHIE. You want to be changed for life?

TOM. Who doesn't?

SOPHIE. Then sit down again.

TOM. No, I'll be off now. I think I'm a bit mad sometimes: honest.

SOPHIE. Sit, please.

TOM. No, really—

SOPHIE. (*Sharp.*) Look, mister, what kind of a gentleman are you? You come here to ask my advice. I settle myself to give it. Then without a word of respect you turn your back and go!

TOM. You *told* me to go!

SOPHIE. Don't argue with a Baroness! Why do you people have no breeding?

TOM. I'm sorry—

SOPHIE. Then sit!

(*Bewildered,* TOM *hangs up his coat again.*)

Look, mister. Just for a giggle—you with your paleness—me with my headache—why don't we explore a little the possibility of changing your life? All right?

TOM. (*Sitting.*) All right.

SOPHIE. I'll tell you a little your past, a little your present: then your future. (SHE *stares into the ball.*) Mmm. It's very disturbed. There's much confusion . . . 1945. You were born in 1945?

TOM. (*Surprised.*) Yes!

SOPHIE. It's very ritualistic, the ball. Often first it gives the date of birth, then the place . . . Ja! Exactly! . . . Ah! I see now a place. A dirty street. A little narrow house: brown: wet: working-class. Somewhere in the North, maybe . . . In the

[27]

background a huge wheel turning. A coal mine! Ja—a coal village.

(TOM *reacts to this, very startled.*)

I see I'm not too far from the truth. There's no woman in the house. Your mother is dead, ja? . . . Your father still alive. At least I see a man in working clothes—bad face— brutal face—heavy, like a drunk man.

(HE *stares at her, riveted.*)

And what's this now? I see a child. A little pale face—Pale! Eyes frightened. Oh, mister, no! Such a frightened face! . . . He ill-treated you?

(SHE *stares at him.* HE *looks away quickly.*)

Beat you, ja? . . . I must look closer here . . . What's this now? A fire. On it I see something, burning.

TOM. (*Nervously.*) What? . . . What? . . .

SOPHIE. A guitar. Can it be a guitar? . . . What is it? A symbol perhaps of your music talent?

(TOM *rises, terrified.*)

I disturb you, mister?

TOM. You saw *that?* . . .

SOPHIE. Very plain.

TOM. No—it's impossible. It *is!* . . .

SOPHIE. I'm sorry. It was absolutely clear.

TOM. You can't. Just—not! . . . My head—It's here!

SOPHIE. And for me, it's there. You can lock nothing away, my dear. Time that happened once for you, happens now for me . . . Why did he do that? To stop you being a musician? . . . To hurt you? . . .

(TOM, *who has been walking up and down the room, suddenly stops, and stands rigid, struck by something.*)

What is it? Perhaps I should stop now?

TOM. No . . . Go on . . .

SOPHIE. You are upset.

TOM. Doesn't matter . . . It's what I'm paying for, after all.

SOPHIE. I stop.

TOM. (*Urgently.*) No! What else do you see?

(SOPHIE *stares at him: then returns to the ball.*)

SOPHIE. Ah: it's better now. Happiness I think is coming. I see a dot of bright pink, moving toward me. It's a girl. On her head a pink scarf. Very pretty: a blonde girl. You know her?

TOM. Go on.

SOPHIE. Now I see you. She is running to you—you reach out to stop her—but no: she runs right past you. Beloved God!

TOM. What?

SOPHIE. There's someone else. A man. I can't see his face. He wears a green jacket in corduroy. He puts out his hand. She takes it. (*Pause.*) They walk away together—leaving you alone.

TOM. Alone.

SOPHIE. Ja. The alone of alone. More alone than I've ever seen it.

TOM. (*Dead.*) So that's the message. "Alone."

SOPHIE. Does this make sense to you, mister?

TOM. Oh yes. It makes sense. It makes sense . . . (*More to himself.*) What a way to do it!

SOPHIE. To do what, please?

TOM. What a crazy way! To arrange all this—just to let me know! . . . I suppose he set it up as a little joke!

SOPHIE. Who, please?

TOM. No, he could hardly expect you to do it for free. Then it was a few quid on the side.

SOPHIE. What d'you mean?

TOM. Christ, he's crazy! He must be!—

SOPHIE. Young mister, are you suggesting I've been bribed?

TOM. No, I'm not suggesting it. I'm saying it.

SOPHIE. How dare you? How absolutely bloody dare you?

TOM. Because I absolutely know, that's why. There's only one person I've ever told about my childhood—and that's Frank. So, you see.

SOPHIE. My dear, to a professional eye like mine, truth does not have to be told. It is evident.

TOM. I daresay. And what if it isn't the truth?

(A *long pause between them.*)

SOPHIE. I beg your pardon?

TOM. What if it's a zonking great lie . . . Like every word of that story.

(*Pause.*)

SOPHIE. I don't believe it . . .

TOM. It's true.

SOPHIE. Impossible. You say this to discredit me.

TOM. Why should I do that?

SOPHIE. Look, mister, what I see, I see. Lemberg never lies!

TOM. No—but I *do* . . . The bit with the guitar I invented as late as last week.

SOPHIE. You mean your father is not a miner?

TOM. No. He's a very nice accountant, living up in Hoylake.

SOPHIE. And your mother isn't dead?

TOM. Not in the biological sense, no. She likes her game of golf and gives bridge parties every Wednesday.

SOPHIE. But your accent . . .

TOM. (*Letting it drop.*) I'm afraid that's as put on as everything else. I mean, there's no point changing your background if you're going to keep your accent, is there?

SOPHIE. Beloved God!

TOM. Actually, it slips a bit when I'm drunk, but people just think I'm being affected.

SOPHIE. You mean to say . . . you live your whole life like this. One enormous lie from morning to night?

TOM. I suppose I do.

SOPHIE. Unimaginable!

TOM. Does it worry you?

SOPHIE. Doesn't it worry *you*?

TOM. Sometimes, yes. But not all the time. I've got used to it, I suppose. I regard the whole thing as a sort of . . .

SOPHIE. White lie?

TOM. Yes—very good. A white lie!

SOPHIE. But why? Why? WHY in heaven's name?

TOM. Well, it started as a question of image really. I mean I quickly found out in the world of pop music you've got to be working class to get anywhere. Middle class is right out. No one believes you can sing with the authentic voice of the people if you're the son of an accountant. I mean, sweat's O.K., but taxes turn people off. Do you dig?

SOPHIE. Are you serious?

TOM. Believe me, Baroness: I've worked it out. Look—everyone makes images—*everyone*. It's like no one can look at anyone direct. The way I see it, the whole world's made up of images —images talking at images—that's what makes it all so impossible!

SOPHIE. And do your parents know you've worked it out like this? Disowning them completely?

TOM. No. But they might as well. They've virtually disowned me, after all. Dad calls me "Minstrel Boy" now every time I go home, and mother has a whole bit with her bridge club that I'm in London "studying" music. Studying is a better *image* than singing in clubs. She can *see* herself as the mother of a student. Both of them are talking about themselves, of course, not me. And I don't blame them. That's what I'm doing too. And all of us . . .

SOPHIE. What a complicated young mister you are.

TOM. Do you think I'm a bit mad?

SOPHIE. Because you choose to be somebody else? No, that's not mad. That's not mad. Not entirely.

TOM. I've never told anyone this before. You must have very special powers.

SOPHIE. Can you really believe that after the way I told your fortune?

TOM. Well you were pretending then.

SOPHIE. If I were any good, my dear, would I need to pretend? Oh come: it's me to be embarrassed, not you. It serves me right for playing silly games. Let's have a drink—what do you say? Cheer us both up!

TOM. I think it's more than a game to him.

(SHE *rises and goes to the sideboard.*)

SOPHIE. Why?

TOM. Well, he's always pulling gags, but he's never gone this far before. He can be really marvelous when he wants to. And then there's another side of him—like this . . . all right, he's guessed about me and Helen—this is still a pretty weird way of telling me, isn't it? Is that all he asked you to say to me? That I was alone?

SOPHIE. (*Avoiding him.*) Mister, please have a drink. I always take a glass of retsina about this hour in the afternoon. It tastes like gasoline, but it can be very encouraging.

TOM. Thank you. I think I will.

SOPHIE. My husband would never let me drink when he was alive. Mind you, he managed a luxury hotel—so he had to be . . . careful.

[32]

TOM. It's so strange his coming here like this. What does he think's going on between Helen and me?

SOPHIE. You feel very strongly about this girl?

TOM. Yes.

SOPHIE. And she about you?

TOM. That's part of it.

(SHE *hands him his drink.*)

SOPHIE. Are you afraid of him?

TOM. I don't know.

SOPHIE. Is she?

TOM. Maybe, I think so, yes.

SOPHIE. Well, that makes three of us.

TOM. You don't know what it can be like sometimes in that house.

SOPHIE. You all three live together?

TOM. Yes. Me upstairs, them down. I wake up every morning thinking of her in his bed. When I come downstairs, he lies there smiling at me.

SOPHIE. Why don't you leave?

TOM. I can't.

SOPHIE. Why not?

TOM. I can't. Isn't it incredible? And every morning I get up and play that part: the coal miner's son frying up breakfast for three! And avoiding her eyes—her great green eyes.

SOPHIE. You mean you haven't even told her the truth?

TOM. Why should I? The real me, as they say, isn't a wow with women. Look! Truth's the last thing she wants. She's "in love"—that's what she calls it! She's in love with a working class boy—even though he doesn't exist. And I'm in love with feelings I see in her eyes—and I know they don't exist. They're only what I read into them. I tell you that's what it's all about—images making noises at images: love!—love!—

love!—love!—(*Pause.*) Love. God, you should see those eyes . . .

SOPHIE. Ja?

TOM. They're amazing! Like you said, the alone of alone. Well, these are the green of green.

SOPHIE. Eyes. It's always the eyes.

TOM. I don't know why I'm telling you all this.

SOPHIE. Green or black, it's always the same.

(SHE *rises and moves slowly to the photograph.*)

TOM. I can stretch out quite still for hours, and imagine I'm lying at the bottom of her eyes.

SOPHIE. With me it was black. Immense black, like the olives.

TOM. Like lying on the bottom of the sea, staring up . . .

SOPHIE. (*Gazing at the photograph.*) He said to me once: "A Greek proverb for you, Sophie. 'Black eyes are the olives at the feast of love.'" (*Looking at the photograph.*) He made it up, of course.

TOM. Who?

SOPHIE. Someone who was lied to.

TOM. He's got a marvelous face.

SOPHIE. Oh yes, white—quite white—with eyes stuck in it so huge. Like an icon of honesty. I remember the first time I saw him I thought: "Beloved God, he's dying!" He was paler even than you. He stood on my doorstep with a little suitcase in his hand, full of white shirts and a history of the Tudor kings. He was so polite and thin—like a breathing match-stick—like you—and he bowed so formal. "My name is Vassili. I am a student from Greece. Do you have a room, please? I regret I cannot pay more than three pounds."

TOM. When was this?

SOPHIE. Five years ago. I was a landlady then in Notting Hill. My husband had died penniless: I had to do something be-

sides tell fortunes. Oh well—other years, other tears! . . .
He was twenty-six years old, but still exactly like a child.
Everything he felt, he gave you, like a present—*shoved* at
you, a joy now, another joy, all day. He used to come into
my room in the evening to watch the television. Always so
neat and careful. "Excuse me, is there rock and roll entertainment tonight?" Now *there* was a fan! He taught me
everything: what groups were good, what lousy, Top Ten,
Pick of the Pops! Secretly I liked it, but it was vulgar to
admit to. After all, I was the Baroness Lemberg. His own
family was just middle class. They sent him what they could,
but it wasn't much. In a while I stopped asking him for rent
. . . and he spent the money instead on pink sweets, yellow
beads, tributes to his lady. He lived for dancing and history!
He was absolutely intoxicated by history! And because I was
an aristocrat, you see, I was supposed to know all about it.
Every Sunday we went on a bus—up to Windsor Castle,
down to St. Paul's Cathedral. And what he never knew was
that every Saturday night I would sit up, secretly memoriz-
ing the facts—then speaking them next day, almost yawning,
because tourism, after all, is a little common, my dear . . .
Typically I never looked at the buildings themselves. Only
their reflections in his eyes. So one bright spring day, I
saw St. Paul's—two tiny little cathedrals swimming in salt
water—and I leaned forward and kissed them, and called him
"Mein Liebe" for the first time.

(*Pause.*)

Can it be you have powers for me too—to make me say
things? . . .

TOM. Go on.

SOPHIE. Well . . . all along there was a fiancée. Her name was
Irina—a slouchy little thing, living with her parents in Lon-

don. She had been chosen for him by the two fathers, who were best friends. Do you know they still do things like that in Greece? He was allowed to take her for walks in the afternoon, but nothing more for two years, till he had finished his studies and could marry. Well, over the months, just because he was forbidden to touch her, he started to whine. "Oh Sophie, I need her so bad. Help me, help me!" And I—because it was so vulgar, you see, to show jealousy —I said to him—

TOM. "Invite her home."

SOPHIE. (*Surprised.*) Ja! . . . "Secretly to your room, in the afternoon. If there are any questions, I shall have been chaperone."

TOM. And she came, of course.

SOPHIE. Every week!

TOM. And you?

SOPHIE. I served them tea . . . into their room with my little tray.

(SHE *picks up the photograph and bears it like a tray over to the table.*)

"Hello, Irina: How are you? How well you look! How's your good father?" And underneath, the *hate!* I, who had never felt hate in my life before, *wasted* its first flood on her; a little *nothing* who never harmed me! Oh, that hate. Burning me so I would cry out to the wallpaper on the stairs—and then into them immediately—smiling, holding out chocolate biscuits. "Oh, Vassili, don't grab them like that. It's so rude at a lady's tea table!"

(SHE *throws the photograph down onto the table.*)

I was you—frying your breakfasts!

TOM. Yes!

SOPHIE. Oh, mister, what pain comes when you start protecting white lies!

(*The lights spring on outside, red and blue.*

SHE *moves toward the window, talking.*)

Dishonest pain. Pain not earned. Pain like an escape from real pain . . . You know the terrible thing? Even now part of me wishes him unhappy, wherever he is, back in Greece, gulping down ice cream in some café, a bright icon with a child's sweet tooth. But then part of me wished *me* unhappy, and who can explain *that?* Always it escapes me. Though now and then, staring here across the water, I think I see the pattern. Then no. Like wrinkles on the skin of the sea, a cold wind rushes up and it dissolves.

(SHE *stares out of the window.*)

TOM. What happened?

SOPHIE. One day he brought me a present. Him—in his little cage. He said: "Here, Sophie, this is Pericles. In Greece he is known as the bird of truth. No one must ever lie in his presence!" He made that up too—*naturally!* "What do you mean," I say to Vassi, "no one must lie?" He sits down giggling. "Sophie, I was talking to Miss Steinberg, that friend who knew you in Germany before the war. She says you were not a Baroness at all. You were a Jewish girl from a poor family: a refugee who married a horrid Englishman who kept a pub. Not a grand hotel, like you said: a pub. And you were not a manageress in a great office. You were only a barmaid."

TOM. He made that up too?

(*Pause.*)

SOPHIE. No, he didn't . . . (*Pause.*) No.

TOM. I see.

SOPHIE. So now standing there, I am ice all over. "Darling," I

say, very concerned, "it is time we talked. The two years
here are almost up. Our relationship is not fair to Irina. You
must think of your marriage." He smiles back—giving me his
present, so happy! "I *have* thought, Sophie, and I tell you I
do not wish to marry her. I cannot love someone chosen for
me by my father." And now it comes! The Baroness speaks
for the last time! (*Cooing.*) "That's nonsense, Vassili. You
are both young. You are both Greek. You are right together.
If you wish to make me happy—*marry her!*"

TOM. No!

SOPHIE. Right together. Very, very right together!

TOM. But why?

SOPHIE. Because it was in his *face*—don't you see?—*I saw it!*

TOM. Saw?

SOPHIE. *Love!* . . . Not despising! Not anger with me! Just love,
for me!—smiling in those black eyes. Now we were equal!
. . . Now he could *know* me!

(*Pause.*)

Intolerable.

TOM. (*Understanding.*) Yes.

(TOM *gets up, disturbed. There is a long pause.*)

SOPHIE. You asked for the crystal ball.

TOM. I didn't, actually . . . But never mind. (HE *gives her a
smile.*)

SOPHIE. Intolerable . . . And for you too? . . . Are you just
afraid of seeming middle class? . . . I hope so. You want
advice from the witch by the sea? Dare to be known. Dare to
love yourself . . . so much. Go to your girl now. Tell her all
your lies. She will laugh, I promise you.

TOM. And Frank? Will he laugh too?

SOPHIE. What does that matter? You've never really been afraid
of him. Only of yourself. Do you see?

TOM. Yes, maybe! But still—

SOPHIE. What? Still what?

TOM. I owe him everything. When he found me singing in a Chelsea pub, I didn't have a penny to my name. He founded the group . . . he set me up . . . What kind of thanks is it to steal his girl?

SOPHIE. Thanks?!

TOM. Yes—thanks! Is that so funny?

SOPHIE. (*Slowly.*) Mister, do you want to know what your friend really wanted me to see for you in that crystal ball? Him and your girl burning to ashes. His word—ashes . . .

(*Pause.* HE *looks at her in horror.*)

I'm sorry.

TOM. He said that?—You wouldn't lie. Not about this?—

(*The bell sounds outside. Both glance at it mutely.*)

SOPHIE. No, not to you. (*Urgent and low.*) Go to her now, before the concert, take a deep breath—and tell her everything. I'll deal with him.

TOM. How?

SOPHIE. Just go!

(SHE *propels him to the door.*)

I said before you had disbelieving eyes. It's not true. There is still a little hope in them. Don't let it fade out, mister. Like the sky into the sea. All gray.

TOM. Good-bye, Baroness.

SOPHIE. Sophie.

TOM. Sophie.

(*Suddenly* SHE *kisses him on the cheek. They contemplate each other for a second. Then he opens the door.* FRANK *stands on the other side of it.* TOM *brushes by him and out into the night.* FRANK *lounges into the room, shutting the door.*)

FRANK. Tom: It worked, didn't it? What happened, then?

SOPHIE. I read his fortune.

FRANK. (*Excitedly.*) I bet you did! Come on now—give me every detail, right from the beginning. Don't leave anything out!

SOPHIE. Mister, I'm afraid things have not gone quite as planned.

FRANK. What d'you mean?

SOPHIE. Your friend is more complicated than you think.

FRANK. Why? What happened?

SOPHIE. I don't know.

FRANK. Meaning?

SOPHIE. It grew dark. The lights came on.

FRANK. (*Suddenly hard.*) Look, Baroness, I'm in no mood for games. Where was he off to in such a hurry?

SOPHIE. (*Scared.*) Mister, would you like a drink? Look, maybe I tell your fortune . . . for free!

FRANK. Where was he going, Baroness?

SOPHIE. To his concert, naturally!

FRANK. I don't think so . . . You're lying, aren't you?

SOPHIE. No.

FRANK. Oh yes, you're lying . . . There's cheat in this room. I can smell it. It's hanging in the air like smoke . . . Lady, you cheated me.

SOPHIE. No! I did exactly what you said. I earned my money!

FRANK. (*Disbelieving.*) Lady, you cheated me! . . . He's gone off to—tell Helen, hasn't he? To Helen about all this.

SOPHIE. Of course not.

FRANK. To show me up in front of her—to show me up—to show me up . . . (*Violently.*) You cheating old cow!!!

SOPHIE. Cheat? *Me*—cheat? Me! After what you asked me to do! . . . Fantastic! . . . (*Furious.*) Listen, Mister—Mr. Cool and Easy—Mr. Giggle—nobody ever leaves you, do they? Well, news for you! Bloody marvelous news for you. They do—and they will! Tonight! (*Pause.*) You've lost her. But then did you ever really have her?

FRANK. (*Quietly.*) Well, well, well. Who'd have guessed it? Here I was thinking Lemberg may be a bore, but inside that frumpy old bag is a real witch—and all the time she's only a provincial pocket book psychologist. Come on now. Give me back the money.

SOPHIE. No.

FRANK. Come on now. There's a good girl. No witch—no fee. It's fair, you know.

SOPHIE. No!

FRANK. (*Dangerous.*) Hand it over, Baroness.

SOPHIE. No. I need it! I have my rent!

(FRANK *walks deliberately to the cage, reaches in and takes out the bird.*)

FRANK. Last chance, dear. Or no witch—no familiar.

(*Silence. Then:*)

SOPHIE. (*Shouting.*) No!!

(FRANK *looks at her, then opens the window and throws the bird out into the wind.* SOPHIE *shrieks.* THEY *face each other.*)

FRANK. A bird for a bird.

(*A pause.*)

SOPHIE. (*Icy.*) I regret you do not frighten me, sir. Not one hour ago in this room I told Pericles that he would be going on a long, long journey! Perhaps I am not so much a fake, after all.

FRANK. (*Ironically.*) Very brave, Baroness. Very brave and gallant. (*Hard.*) Now—the money.

SOPHIE. I am not a Baroness, mister. My name is Sophie Harburg. And maybe I am not a witch of Endor, but I can still read you. For free.

(SHE *sits, slowly, looking at him.*)

You want your money? Very well.

(SHE *extracts the money from her blouse, takes off the rubber band, and proceeds to deal out the notes onto the table in front of him as if they were cards.*)

Five of pounds: card of cruelty. Five of pounds: card of vanity. Five of pounds: card of stupidity. Five of pounds: card of fantasy. Five of pounds:—card of a loveless life. It's all in the cards, mister.

(HE *stares at her. Then with a swift gesture, sweeps up the notes and leaves the parlor, shutting the door hard behind him. Left alone,* SOPHIE *sits a moment, then reaches out for the photograph lying on the table.*

To Vassili.)

Harburg never lies.

(SHE *drops the photograph gently on the floor, discarding it.*)

Never.

(SHE *stares out at the gathering evening.*)

CURTAIN

IN MEMORY OF
Jerry Weinstein
WHO LAUGHED

Characters

BRINDSLEY MILLER: *A young sculptor (mid-twenties), intelligent and attractive, but nervous and uncertain of himself.*

CAROL MELKETT: *His fiancée. A young debutante; very pretty, very spoiled; very silly. Her sound is that unmistakable, terrifying deb quack.*

MISS FURNIVAL: *A middle-aged spinster. Prissy; and refined. Clad in the blouse and sack skirt of her gentility, her hair in a bun, her voice in a bun, she reveals only the repressed gestures of the middle-class spinster—until alcohol undoes her.*

COLONEL MELKETT: CAROL's *commanding father. Brisk, barky, yet given to sudden vocal calms which suggest a deep and alarming instability. It is not only the constant darkness which gives him his look of wide-eyed suspicion.*

HAROLD GORRINGE: *The camp owner of an antique-china shop, and* BRINDSLEY's *neighbor,* HAROLD *comes from the North of England. His friendship is highly conditional and possessive: sooner or later, payment for it will be asked. A specialist in emotional blackmail, he can become hysterical when slighted, or (as inevitably happens) rejected. He is older than* BRINDSLEY *by several years.*

SCHUPPANZIGH: *A middle-class German refugee, chubby, cultivated, and effervescent. He is an entirely happy man, delighted to be in England, even if this means being employed full time by the London Electricity Board.*

CLEA: BRINDSLEY's *ex-mistress. Mid-twenties; dazzling, emo-*

tional, bright and mischievous. The challenge to her to create a dramatic situation out of the darkness is ultimately irresistible.

GEORG BAMBERGER: *An elderly millionaire art collector, easily identifiable as such.*

THE SET: *The action of the play takes place in* BRINDSLEY'S *apartment in South Kensington, London. This forms the ground floor of a large house now divided into flats.* HAROLD GORRINGE *lives opposite;* MISS FURNIVAL *lives above.*

There are four ways out of the room. A door at the left, up-stage, leads directly across the passage to HAROLD'S *room. The door to this, with its mat laid tidily outside, can clearly be seen. A curtain, upstage center, screens* BRINDSLEY'S *studio: when it is parted we glimpse samples of his work in metal. To the right of this an open stair shoots steeply up to his bedroom above, reached through a door at the top. To the left, downstage, a trap in the floor leads down to the cellar.*

It is a gay room, when we finally see it, full of color and space and new shapes. It is littered with marvelous objects— mobiles, mannikins, toys, and dotty bric-a-brac—the happy paraphernalia of a free and imaginative mind. The total effect is of chaos tidied in honor of an occasion, and of a temporary elegance created by the furniture borrowed from HAROLD GOR-RINGE *and arranged to its best advantage.*

This consists of three elegant Regency chairs in gold leaf; a Regency chaise-longue to match; a small Queen Anne table bearing a fine opaline lamp, with a silk shade; a Wedgwood bowl in black basalt; a good Coalport vase containing summer flowers; and a fine porcelain Buddha.

The only things which actually belong to BRINDSLEY *are a cheap square table bearing the drinks; an equally cheap round*

*table in the middle of the room, shrouded by a cloth and deco-
rated with the Wedgwood bowl; a low stool downstage center,
improved by the Buddha; a record player; and his own artistic
creations. These are largely assumed to be in the studio await-
ing inspection; but one of them is visible in this room. On the
dais stands a bizarre iron sculpture dominated by two long
detachable metal prongs, and hung with metal pieces which
jangle loudly if touched. On the wall hang paintings, some of
them presumably by* CLEA. *All are non-figurative: colorful geo-
metric designs, splashes, splodges and splats of color; whirls
and whorls and wiggles—all testifying more to a delight in
handling paint than to an ability to achieve very much with it.*

THE TIME: 9:30 *on a Sunday night.*

THE LIGHT: *On the few occasions when a lighter is lit,
matches are struck or a torch is put on, the light on stage
merely gets dimmer. When these objects are extinguished, the
stage immediately grows brighter.*

COMPLETE DARKNESS.

Two voices are heard: BRINDSLEY *and* CAROL. THEY *must give
the impression of two people walking round a room with absolute confidence, as if in the light. We hear sounds as of furniture being moved. A chair is dumped down.*

BRINDSLEY. There! How do you think the room looks?
CAROL. (*Quacking.*) Fabulous! I wish you could always have it
   like this. That lamp looks divine there. And those chairs are
   just the right color. I told you green would look well in here.
BRINDSLEY. Suppose Harold comes back?
CAROL. He is not coming back till tomorrow morning.

   (BRINDSLEY *paces nervously.*)

BRINDSLEY. I know. But suppose he comes tonight? He's mad about his antiques. What do you think he'll say if he goes into his room and finds out we've stolen them?

CAROL. Don't dramatize. We haven't stolen all his furniture. Just three chairs, the sofa, that table, the lamp, the bowl, and the vase of flowers, that's all.

BRINDSLEY. And the Buddha. That's more valuable than anything. Look at it.

CAROL. Oh, do stop worrying, darling.

BRINDSLEY. Well, you don't know Harold. He won't even let anyone touch his antiques.

CAROL. Look, we'll put everything back as soon as Mr. Bamberger leaves. Now stop being dreary.

BRINDSLEY. Well, frankly, I don't think we should have done it. I mean—*anyway*, Harold or no.

CAROL. Why not, for heaven's sake? The room looks divine now. Just look at it!

BRINDSLEY. Darling, Georg Bamberger's a multi-millionaire. He's lived all his life against this sort of furniture. Our few stolen bits aren't going to impress him. He's coming to see the work of an unknown sculptor. If you ask me, it would look much better to him if he found me exactly as I really am: a poor artist. It might touch his heart.

CAROL. It might—but it certainly won't impress Daddy. Remember, he's coming too.

BRINDSLEY. As if I could forget! Why you had to invite your monster father tonight, I can't think!

CAROL. Oh, not again!

BRINDSLEY. Well, it's too bloody much. If he's going to be persuaded I'm a fit husband for you, just by watching a famous collector buy some of my work, he doesn't deserve to have me as a son-in-law!

[50]

CAROL. He just wants some proof you can earn your own living.

BRINDSLEY. And what if Bamberger *doesn't* like my work?

CAROL. He will, darling. Just stop worrying.

BRINDSLEY. I can't. Get me a whiskey.

(SHE *does. We hear her steps, and a glass clink against a bottle—then the sound of a soda syphon.*)

I've got a foreboding. It's all going to be a disaster. An A-one, copper-bottomed, twenty-four-carat disaster.

CAROL. Look, darling, you know what they say. Faint heart never won fair ladypegs!

BRINDSLEY. How true.

CAROL. The trouble with you is you're what Daddy calls a Determined Defeatist.

BRINDSLEY. The more I hear about your Daddy, the more I hate him. I loathe military men anyway . . . and in any case, he's bound to hate me.

CAROL. Why?

BRINDSLEY. Because I'm a complete physical coward. He'll smell it on my breath.

CAROL. Look, darling, all you've got to do is stand up to him. Daddy's only a bully when he thinks people are afraid of him.

BRINDSLEY. Well, I am.

CAROL. You haven't even met him.

BRINDSLEY. That doesn't make any difference.

CAROL. Don't be ridiculous. (*Hands him a drink.*) Here.

BRINDSLEY. Thanks.

CAROL. What can he do? To you?

BRINDSLEY. For one thing, he can refuse to let me marry you.

CAROL. Ah, that's sweetipegs.

(THEY *embrace.*)

BRINDSLEY. I like you in yellow. It brings out your hair.

CAROL. Straighten your tie. You look sloppy.

BRINDSLEY. Well, you look divine.

CAROL. Really?

BRINDSLEY. I mean it. I've never seen you look so lovely.

CAROL. Tell me, Brin, have there been many before me?

BRINDSLEY. Thousands.

CAROL. Seriously!

BRINDSLEY. Seriously—none.

CAROL. What about that girl in the photo?

BRINDSLEY. She lasted about three months.

CAROL. When?

BRINDSLEY. Two years ago.

CAROL. What was her name?

BRINDSLEY. Clea.

CAROL. What was she like?

BRINDSLEY. She was a painter. Very honest. Very clever. And just about as cozy as a steel razor blade.

CAROL. When was the last time you saw her?

BRINDSLEY. (*Evasively.*) I told you . . . two years ago.

CAROL. Well, why did you still have her photo in your bedroom drawer?

BRINDSLEY. It was just there. That's all. Give me a kiss . . . (*Pause.*) No one in the world kisses like you.

CAROL. (*Murmuring.*) Tell me something . . . did you like it better with her—or me?

BRINDSLEY. Like what?

CAROL. Sexipegs.

BRINDSLEY. Look, people will be here in a minute. Put a record on. It had better be something for your father. What does he like?

CAROL. (*Crossing to the record player.*) He doesn't like anything except military marches.

[52]

BRINDSLEY. I might have guessed . . . Wait—I think I've got some! That last record on the shelf. The orange cover. It's called "Marching and Murdering with Sousa," or something.

CAROL. This one?

BRINDSLEY. That's it.

CAROL. (*Getting it.*) "The Band of the Coldstream Guards."

BRINDSLEY. Ideal. Put it on.

CAROL. How d'you switch on?

BRINDSLEY. The last knob on the left. That's it . . . Let us pray! Oh God, let this evening go all right! Let Mr. Bamberger like my sculpture and buy some! Let Carol's monster father like me! And let my neighbor Harold Gorringe never find out that we borrowed his precious furniture behind his back! Amen.

(*A Sousa march; loud. Hardly has it begun, however, when it runs down—as if there is a failure of electricity.*

BRILLIANT LIGHT FLOODS THE STAGE. THE REST OF THE PLAY, SAVE FOR THE TIMES WHEN MATCHES ARE STRUCK, OR FOR THE SCENE WITH SCHUPPANZIGH, IS ACTED IN THIS LIGHT, BUT AS IF IN PITCH DARKNESS.

THEY *freeze:* CAROL *by the end of the sofa;* BRINDSLEY *by the drinks table. The* GIRL's *dress is a silk flag of chic wrapped round her greyhound's body. The* BOY's *look is equally cool: narrow, contained, and sexy. Throughout the evening, as things slide into disaster for him, his crisp, detached shape degenerates progressively into sweat and rumple—just as the elegance of his room gives way relentlessly to its usual near-slum appearance. For the place, as for its owner, the evening is a progress through disintegration.*)

God! We've blown a fuse!

(*The structure and appearance of* BRINDSLEY's *room is described in the note at the beginning of the play.*)

CAROL. *Oh no!*

BRINDSLEY. It must be. (HE *blunders to the light switch, feeling ahead of him, trying to part the darkness with his hands. Finding the switch,* HE *flicks it on and off.*)

CAROL. It is!

BRINDSLEY. Oh no!

CAROL. Or a power cut. Where's the box?

BRINDSLEY. In the hall.

CAROL. Have you any candles?

BRINDSLEY. No. Damn!

CAROL. Where are the matches?

BRINDSLEY. They should be on the drinks table. (*Feeling round the bottles.*) No. Try on the record player.

(THEY *both start groping about the room, feeling for matches.*)

Damn, damn, damn, damn, damn, damn!

(CAROL *sets a maraca rattling off the record player.*)

CAROL. There! (*Finding it.*) No . . .

(*The telephone rings.*)

BRINDSLEY. Would you believe it?!

(HE *blunders his way toward the sound of the bell. Just in time* HE *remembers the central table—and stops himself colliding into it with a smile of self-congratulation.*)

All right: I'm coming!

(*Instead* HE *trips over the dais, and goes sprawling—knocking the phone onto the floor.* HE *has to grope for it on his knees, hauling the receiver back to him by the wire. Into receiver.*)

Hallo? . . . (*In sudden horror.*) Hallo! . . . No, no, no, no— I'm fine, just fine! . . . You? . . . (*His hand over the receiver: to* CAROL.) Darling—look in the bedroom, will you?

CAROL. I haven't finished in here yet.

BRINDSLEY. Well, I've just remembered there's some fuse wire in the bedroom. In that drawer where you found the photograph. Go and get it, will you?

CAROL. I don't think there is. I didn't see any there.

BRINDSLEY. (*Snapping.*) Don't argue. Just look!

CAROL. All right. Keep your hairpiece on.

(*During the following* SHE *gropes her way cautiously up the stairs—head down, arms up the banisters, silken bottom thrust out with the effort.*)

BRINDSLEY. (*Controlling himself.*) I'm sorry. I just know it's there, that's all. You must have missed it.

CAROL. What about the matches?

BRINDSLEY. We'll have to mend it in the dark, that's all. Please hurry, dear.

CAROL. (*Climbing.*) Oh God, how dreary!

BRINDSLEY. (*Taking his hand off the receiver and listening to hear* CAROL *go.*) Hallo? . . . Well, well, well, well! How are you? Good. That's just fine. Fine, fine! . . . Stop saying what?

(CAROL *reaches the top of the stairs—and from force of habit pulls down her skirt before groping her way into the bedroom.*)

BRINDSLEY. (*Hand still over the receiver.*) Carol? . . . Darling? . . .

(*Satisfied* SHE *has gone; in a rush into the telephone, his voice low.*)

Clea! What are you doing here? I thought you were in Finland . . . But you've hardly been gone six weeks . . . Where are you speaking from? . . . The Air Terminal? . . . Well, no, that's not a good idea tonight. I'm terribly busy, and I'm afraid I just can't get out of it. It's business.

CAROL. (*Calling from the bedroom door, above.*) There's nothing there except your dreary socks. I told you.

BRINDSLEY. (*Calling back.*) Well, try the other drawers . . . (HE *rises as* HE *speaks, turning so that the wire wraps itself around his legs.*

CAROL *returns to her search.*

Low and rapid, into phone.)

Look: I can't talk now. Can I call you tomorrow? Where will you be? . . . Look, I told you *no*, Clea. Not tonight. I know it's just around the corner, that's not the point. You can't come round . . . Look, the situation's changed. Something's happened this past month—

CAROL. (*Off.*) I can't see anything. Brin, *please!*—

BRINDSLEY. Clea, I've got to go . . . Look, I can't discuss it over the phone . . . Has it got to do with what? Yes, of course it has. I mean you can't expect things to stay frozen, can you?

CAROL. (*Emerging from the bedroom.*) There's nothing here. Haven't we any matches at all?

BRINDSLEY. Oh stop wailing! (*Into phone.*) No, not you. I'll call you tomorrow. Good-bye.

(HE *hangs up sharply—but fails to find the rest of the telephone so that* HE *bangs the receiver hard on the table first. Then* HE *has to disentangle himself from the wire. Already* BRINDSLEY *is beginning to be fussed.*)

CAROL. (*Descending.*) Who was that?

BRINDSLEY. Just a chum. Did you find the wire?

CAROL. I can't find anything in this. We've *got* to get some matches!—

BRINDSLEY. I'll try the pub. Perhaps they'll have some candles as well.

[56]

(*Little screams are heard approaching from above. It is* MISS FURNIVAL *groping her way down in a panic.*)

MISS FURNIVAL. (*Squealing.*) Help! Help! . . . Oh please someone help me!

BRINDSLEY. (*Calling out.*) Is that you, Miss Furnival?

MISS FURNIVAL. Mr. Miller? . . .

BRINDSLEY. Yes?

MISS FURNIVAL. Mr. Miller!

BRINDSLEY. Yes!

(SHE *gropes her way in.* BRINDSLEY *crosses to find her, but narrowly misses her.*)

MISS FURNIVAL. Oh, thank God, you're there; I'm so frightened!

BRINDSLEY. Why? Have your lights gone too?

MISS FURNIVAL. Yes!

BRINDSLEY. It must be a power cut. (HE *finds her hand and leads her to the chair downstage left.*)

MISS FURNIVAL. I don't think so. The street lights are on in the front. I saw them from the landing.

BRINDSLEY. Then it must be the main switch of the house.

CAROL. Where is that?

(MISS FURNIVAL *gasps at the strange voice.*)

BRINDSLEY. It's in the cellar. It's all sealed up. No one's allowed to touch it but the electricity people.

CAROL. What are we going to do?

BRINDSLEY. Get them—quick!

CAROL. Will they come at this time of night?

BRINDSLEY. They've got to.

(BRINDSLEY *accidentally touches* MISS FURNIVAL*'s breasts.* SHE *gives a little scream.* BRINDSLEY *gropes his way to the phone.*)

Have you by any chance got a match on you, Miss Furnival?

MISS FURNIVAL. I'm afraid I haven't. So improvident of me. And I'm absolutely terrified of the dark.

BRINDSLEY. Darling, this is Miss Furnival, from upstairs. Miss Furnival—Miss Melkett.

MISS FURNIVAL. How do you do?

CAROL. (*Extending her hand into the darkness.*) How do you do?

MISS FURNIVAL. Isn't this frightful?

(BRINDSLEY *picks up the phone and dials "O".*)

CAROL. Perhaps we can put Mr. Bamberger off.

BRINDSLEY. Impossible. He's dining out and coming on here after. He can't be reached.

CAROL. Oh, flip!

BRINDSLEY. (*Sitting on the dais, and speaking into the phone.*) Hallo, Operator, can you give me the London Electricity Board, please? Night Service . . . I'm sure it's in the book, Miss, but I'm afraid I can't see . . . There's no need to apologize. No, I'm not blind!—I just can't see: we've got a fuse . . . No we *haven't* got any matches! (*Desperate.*) Miss, *please*: this is an emergency . . . Thank you! . . . (*To the room.*) London is staffed with imbeciles!

MISS FURNIVAL. Oh, you're so right, Mr. Miller.

BRINDSLEY. (*Rising, frantic: into the phone.*) Miss, I *don't want* the number: I can't dial it! . . . Well, have *you* ever tried to dial a number in the dark? . . . (*Trying to keep control.*) I just want to be connected . . . Thank you. (*To* MISS FURNIVAL.) Miss Furnival, do you by any remote chance have any candles?

MISS FURNIVAL. I'm afraid not, Mr. Miller.

BRINDSLEY. (*Mouthing nastily at her.*) "I'm afraid not, Mr. Miller" . . . (*Briskly, into phone.*) Hallo? Look, I'd like to report a main fuse at Eighteen Scarlatti Gardens. My name is Miller. (*Exasperated.*) Yes, yes! All right! . . . (*Maddened: to the room.*) Hold on! Hold bloody on!

MISS FURNIVAL. If I might suggest—Harold Gorringe opposite might have some candles. He's away for the weekend, but always leaves his key under the mat.

BRINDSLEY. What a good idea. That's just the sort of practical thing he would have. (*To* CAROL.) Here—take this . . . I'll go and see, love.

(HE *hands her the telephone in a fumble—then makes for the door—only to collide smartly with his sculpture.*)
Bugger!

MISS FURNIVAL. Are you all right, Mr. Miller?

BRINDSLEY. I knew it! I bloody knew it. This is going to be the worst night of my life! . . . (HE *collides with the door.*)

CAROL. Don't panic, darling. Just don't panic!

(HE *stumbles out and is seen groping under* HAROLD's *mat for the key.* HE *finds it and enters the room opposite.*)

MISS FURNIVAL. You're so right, Miss Melkett. We must none of us panic.

CAROL. (*On the phone.*) Hallo? Hallo? (*To* MISS FURNIVAL.) This would have to happen tonight. It's just Brindsley's luck.

MISS FURNIVAL. Is it something special tonight then, Miss Melkett?

CAROL. It couldn't be more special if it tried.

MISS FURNIVAL. Oh, dear. May I ask why?

CAROL. Have you ever heard of a German called Georg Bamberger?

MISS FURNIVAL. Indeed, yes. Isn't he the richest man in the world?

CAROL. Yes. (*Into phone.*) Hallo? . . . (*To* MISS FURNIVAL.) Well, he's coming here tonight.

MISS FURNIVAL. Tonight!

CAROL. In about twenty minutes, to be exact. And to make
matters worse, he's apparently stone deaf.

MISS FURNIVAL. How extraordinary! May I ask why he's coming?

CAROL. He saw some photos of Brindsley's work and apparently
got madly excited about it. His secretary rang up last week
and asked if he could come and see it. He's a great collector.
Brin would be absolutely *made* if Bamberger bought a piece
of his.

MISS FURNIVAL. Oh, how exciting!

CAROL. It's his big break. Or was—till a moment ago.

MISS FURNIVAL. Oh my dear, you *must* get some help. Jiggle
that thing.

CAROL. (*Jiggling the phone.*) *Hallo? Hallo?* . . . Perhaps the
Bomb's fallen, and everyone's dead.

MISS FURNIVAL. Oh, please don't say things like that—even in
levity.

CAROL. (*Someone answers her at last.*) Hallo? Ah! This is
Number Eighteen, Scarlatti Gardens. I'm afraid we've had
the most dreary fuse. It's what's laughingly known as the
Main Switch. We want a *little man* . . . Well, they can't all
have flu . . . Oh, please try! It's screamingly urgent . . .
Thank you. (SHE *hangs up.*) Sometime this evening, they
hope. That's a lot of help.

MISS FURNIVAL. They're not here to help, my dear. In my
young days you paid your rates and you got satisfaction.
Nowadays you just get some foreigner swearing at you. And
if they think you're of the middle class, that only makes it
worse.

CAROL. Would you like a drink?

MISS FURNIVAL. I don't drink, thank you. My dear father, being
a Baptist minister, strongly disapproved of alcohol.

(A *scuffle is heard amongst milk bottles off, followed by a
stifled oath.*)

COLONEL MELKETT. (*Off.*) Damn and blast!! . . . (*Barking.*) Is there anybody there?

CAROL. (*Calling.*) In here, daddypegs!

COLONEL. Can't you put the light on, dammit? I've almost knocked meself out on a damn milk bottle.

CAROL. We've got a fuse. Nothing's working.

(COLONEL MELKETT *appears, holding a lighter which evidently is working—we can see the flame, and of course, the lights go down a little.*)

MISS FURNIVAL. Oh what a relief! A light!

CAROL. This is my father, Colonel Melkett, Miss Furnival. She's from upstairs.

COLONEL. Good evening.

MISS FURNIVAL. I'm taking refuge for a moment with Mr. Miller. I'm not very good in the dark.

COLONEL. When did this happen?

(MISS FURNIVAL, *glad for the light, follows it pathetically as the* COLONEL *crosses the room.*)

CAROL. Five minutes ago. The main just blew.

COLONEL. And where's this young man of yours?

CAROL. In the flat opposite. He's trying to find candles.

COLONEL. You mean he hasn't got any?

CAROL. No. We can't even find the matches.

COLONEL. I see. No organization. Bad sign!

CAROL. Daddy, please. It could happen to any of us.

COLONEL. Not to me.

(HE *turns to find* MISS FURNIVAL *right behind him and glares at her balefully. The poor* WOMAN *retreats to the sofa and sits down.*

COLONEL MELKETT *gets his first sight of* BRINDSLEY'S *sculpture.*)

What the hell's that?

CAROL. Some of Brindsley's work.

COLONEL. Is it, by Jove? And how much does that cost?

CAROL. I think he's asking fifty pounds for it.

COLONEL. My God!

CAROL. (*Nervously.*) Do you like the flat, Daddy? He's furnished it very well, hasn't he? I mean it's rich, but not gaudi-pegs.

COLONEL. Very elegant—good: I can see he's got excellent taste. (*Seeing the Buddha.*) Now that's what I understand by a real work of art—you can see what it's meant to be.

MISS FURNIVAL. Good heavens!

CAROL. What is it?

MISS FURNIVAL. Nothing . . . It's just that Buddha—it so closely resembles the one Harold Gorringe has.

(CAROL *looks panic-stricken.*)

COLONEL. It must have cost a pretty penny, what? He must be quite well off. . . . By Jove—it's got pretty colors. (HE *bends to examine it.*)

CAROL. (*Sotto voce, urgently, to* MISS FURNIVAL.) You know Mr. Gorringe?

MISS FURNIVAL. Oh, very well indeed. We're excellent friends. He has such lovely things . . . (*For the first time* SHE *notices the sofa on which* SHE *is sitting.*) Oh . . .

CAROL. What?

MISS FURNIVAL. This furniture . . . (*Looking about her.*) Surely—?—my goodness!—

CAROL. (*Hastily.*) Daddy, why don't you look in there? It's Brin's studio. There's something I particularly want you to see before he comes back.

COLONEL. What?

CAROL. It—it—er—it's a surprise, go and see.

COLONEL. Very well, Dumpling. Anythin' to oblige. (*To* MISS FURNIVAL.) Excuse me.

(HE *goes off into the studio, taking his lighter with him. The light instantly gets brighter on stage.* CAROL *sits beside the* SPINSTER *on the sofa, crouching like a conspirator.*)

CAROL. (*Low and urgent.*) Miss Furnival, you're a sport, aren't you?

MISS FURNIVAL. I don't know. What is this furniture doing in here? It belongs to Harold Gorringe.

CAROL. I know. We've done something absolutely frightful. We've stolen all his best pieces and put Brin's horrid old bits into *his* room.

MISS FURNIVAL. But why? It's disgraceful!

CAROL. (*Sentimentally.*) Because Brindsley's got nothing, Miss Furnival. Nothing at all. He's as poor as a church mouse. If Daddy had seen this place as it looks normally, he'd have forbidden our marriage on the spot. Mr. Gorringe wasn't there to ask—so we just took the chance.

MISS FURNIVAL. If Harold Gorringe knew that anyone had touched his furniture or his porcelain, he'd go out of his mind! And as for that Buddha—(*Pointing in the wrong direction.*)—it's the most precious piece he owns. It's worth hundreds of pounds.

CAROL. Oh, please, Miss Furnival—you won't give us away, will you? We're desperate! And it's only for an hour . . . Oh, please! *please!*

MISS FURNIVAL. (*Giggling.*) Very well! I won't betray you!

CAROL. Oh, thank you!

MISS FURNIVAL. But it'll have to go back exactly as it was, just as soon as Mr. Bamberger and your father leave.

CAROL. I swear! Oh, Miss Furnival, you're an angel! Do have a drink. Oh no, you don't. Well, have a bitter lemon.

MISS FURNIVAL. Thank you. That I won't refuse.

(*The* COLONEL *returns, still holding his lighter. The stage darkens a little.*)

COLONEL. Well, they're certainly a surprise. And that's supposed to be sculpture?

CAROL. It's not supposed to be. It is.

COLONEL. They'd make good garden implements. I'd like 'em for turnin' the soil.

(MISS FURNIVAL *giggles.*)

CAROL. That's not very funny, Daddy.

(MISS FURNIVAL *stops giggling.*)

COLONEL. Sorry, Dumpling. Speak as you find.

CAROL. I wish you wouldn't call me Dumpling.

COLONEL. Well, there's no point wastin' this. We may need it!

(HE *snaps off his lighter.*

MISS FURNIVAL *gives her little gasp as the stage brightens.*)

CAROL. Don't be nervous, Miss Furnival. Brin will be here in a minute with the candles.

MISS FURNIVAL. Then I'll leave, of course. I don't want to be in your way.

CAROL. You're not at all. (*Hearing him.*) Brin?—

(BRINDSLEY *comes out of* HAROLD's *room—returns the key under the mat.*)

BRINDSLEY. Hallo?

CAROL. Did you find anything?

BRINDSLEY. (*Coming in.*) You can't find anything in this. If there's candles there, *I* don't know where they are. Did you get the electric people?

CAROL. They said they might send someone around later.

BRINDSLEY. How much later?

CAROL. They don't know.

BRINDSLEY. That's a lot of help. What a lookout! Not a bloody candle in the house. A deaf millionaire to show sculpture to—and your monster father to keep happy. Lovely!

COLONEL. (*Grimly lighting his lighter.*) Good evenin'.

(BRINDSLEY *jumps.*)

CAROL. Brin, this *is* my father—Colonel Melkett.

BRINDSLEY. (*Wildly embarrassed.*) Well, well, well, well, well! . . . (*Panic.*) Good evening, sir. Fancy you being there all the time! I—I'm expecting some dreadful neighbors, some neighbor monsters, monster neighbors, you know . . . They rang up and said they might look round . . . Well, well, well . . .

COLONEL. (*Darkly.*) Well, well.

MISS FURNIVAL. (*Nervously.*) Well, well!

CAROL. (*Brightly.*) Well!

(*The* COLONEL *rises and advances on* BRINDSLEY *who retreats before him across the room.*)

COLONEL. You seem to be in a spot of trouble.

BRINDSLEY. (*With mad nervousness.*) Oh, not really! Just a fuse—nothing really, we have them all the time . . . I mean, it won't be the first fuse I've survived, and I daresay it won't be the last! (HE *gives a wild braying laugh.*)

COLONEL. (*Relentless.*) In the meantime, you've got no matches. Right?

BRINDSLEY. Right.

COLONEL. No candles. Right?

BRINDSLEY. Right.

COLONEL. No basic efficiency, right?

BRINDSLEY. I wouldn't say that, exactly . . .

COLONEL. By basic efficiency, young man, I mean the simple state of being At Attention in life, rather than At Ease. Understand?

BRINDSLEY. Well, I'm certainly not at ease.

COLONEL. What are you goin' to do about it?

BRINDSLEY. Do?

COLONEL. Don't echo me, sir. I don't like it.

BRINDSLEY. You don't like it. . . . I'm sorry.

COLONEL. Now look you here. This is an emergency. Anyone can see that.

BRINDSLEY. No one can see anything: that's the emergency. (HE *gives his braying laugh again.*)

COLONEL. Spare me your humor, sir, if you don't mind. Let's look at the situation objectively. Right?

BRINDSLEY. Right.

COLONEL. Good. (HE *snaps off the lighter.*) Problem: Darkness. Solution: Light.

BRINDSLEY. Oh very good, sir.

COLONEL. Weapons: Matches: none! Candles: none! What remains?

BRINDSLEY. Search me.

COLONEL. (*Triumphantly.*) Torches. Torches, sir! what?

BRINDSLEY. Or a set of early Christians.

COLONEL. What did you say?

BRINDSLEY. I'm sorry. I think I'm becoming unhinged. Very good. Torches—brilliant.

COLONEL. Routine. Well, where would you find one?

BRINDSLEY. The pub. What time is it?

(*The* COLONEL *lights his lighter, but now not at the first try. The stage light flickers up and down accordingly.*)

COLONEL. Blasted thing. It's beginnin' to go. (HE *consults his watch.*) Quarter to ten. You can just make it, if you hurry.

BRINDSLEY. Thank you, sir. Your clarity of mind has saved the day.

COLONEL. Well, get on with it, man.

BRINDSLEY. Yes, sir! Back in a minute.

(*The* COLONEL *sits in the Regency chair, downstage right.*)

CAROL. Good luck, darling.

BRINDSLEY. Thank you, my sweet.

(SHE *blows him a kiss.* HE *blows her one back.*)

COLONEL. (*Irritated.*) Stop that at once.

(BRINDSLEY *starts for the door—but as* HE *reaches it,* HAROLD GORRINGE *is heard, off.*)

HAROLD. (*Broad Lancashire accent.*) Hallo? Hallo? Anyone there?

BRINDSLEY. (*Freezing with horror.*) HAROLD!!

HAROLD. Brindsley?

BRINDSLEY. (*Meant for* CAROL.) It's Harold. He's back!

CAROL. Oh no!

BRINDSLEY. THE FURNITURE!!

HAROLD. What's going on here?

(HAROLD *appears.* HE *wears a smart raincoat and carries a weekend suitcase. His hair falls over his brow in a flossy attempt at elegance.*)

BRINDSLEY. Nothing, Harold. Don't go in there—come in here. We've had a fuse. It's dark—it's all over the house.

HAROLD. Have you phoned the electric? (*Reaching out.*)

BRINDSLEY. (*Reaching out and grabbing him.*) Yes. Come in here.

HAROLD. (*Grabbed.*) Ohh! . . . (HE *takes* BRINDSLEY'S *hand and enters the room cozily on his arm.*) It's rather cozy in the dark, isn't it?

BRINDSLEY. (*Desperately.*) Yes! I suppose so . . . So you're back from your weekend then . . .

HAROLD. I certainly am, dear. Weekend! Some weekend! It rained the whole bloody time. I feel damp to my knickers.

BRINDSLEY. (*Nervously.*) Well, have a drink and tell us all about it.

HAROLD. Us? (*Disengaging himself.*) Who's here, then?

MISS FURNIVAL. (*Archly.*) I am, Mr. Gorringe.

HAROLD. Ferny?

MISS FURNIVAL. Taking refuge, I'm afraid. You know how I hate the dark.

COLONEL. (*Attempting to light his lighter.*) Blasted thing! . . . (HE *succeeds.*) There we are! (*Raising it to* GORRINGE's *face, with distaste.*) Who are you?

BRINDSLEY. May I present my neighbor. This is Harold Gorringe—Colonel Melkett.

HAROLD. How do?

COLONEL. How d'ye do?

BRINDSLEY. And this is Miss Carol Melkett, Harold Gorringe.

CAROL. (*Giving him a chilly smile.*) Hallo! . . .

(HAROLD *nods coldly.*)

BRINDSLEY. Here, let me take your raincoat, Harold.

(HE *is wearing a tight, modish, gray suit and a brilliant, strawberry shirt.*)

HAROLD. (*Taking it off and handing it to him.*) Be careful, it's sopping wet.

(*Adroitly,* BRINDSLEY *drops the coat over the Wedgwood bowl on the table.*)

COLONEL. You got no candles, I suppose?

HAROLD. Would you believe it, Colonel, but I haven't? Silly me!

(BRINDSLEY *crosses and blows out the* COLONEL's *lighter, just as* HAROLD *begins to look round the room. The stage brightens.*)

COLONEL. What the devil did you do that for?

BRINDSLEY. I'm saving your wick, Colonel. You may need it later and it's failing fast.

(*The* COLONEL *gives him a suspicious look.* BRINDSLEY *moves quickly back, takes up the coat and drops it over the right end of the sofa, to conceal as much of it as possible.*)

HAROLD. It's all right. I've got some matches.

CAROL. (*Alarmed.*) Matches!

HAROLD. Here we are! I hope I've got the right end. (HE *strikes one.*)

(BRINDSLEY *immediately blows it out from behind, then moves swiftly to hide the Wedgwood bowl under the table and drop the tablecloth over the remaining end of the sofa.* MISS FURNIVAL *sits serenely unknowing between the two covers.*)

Hey, what was that?

BRINDSLEY. (*Babbling.*) A draught. No match stays alight in this room. It's impossible. Cross currents, you know. Old houses are full of them. They're almost a permanent feature in this house . . .

HAROLD. (*Bewildered.*) I don't know what you're on about. (HE *strikes another match.*)

(BRINDSLEY *again blows it out as* HE *nips over to sit in the chair downstage left, but this time is seen.*)

HAROLD. What's up with you?

BRINDSLEY. Nothing!

HAROLD. Have you got a dead body in here or something?

BRINDSLEY. NO! (HE *starts his maniacal laughter.*)

HAROLD. Here, have you been drinking?

BRINDSLEY. No. Of course not.

(HAROLD *strikes another match.* BRINDSLEY *dashes up. All these strikings and blowings are of course accompanied by swift and violent alterations of the light.*)

HAROLD. (*Exasperated.*) Now look here! What's up with you?

BRINDSLEY. (*Inspired.*) Dangerous!

HAROLD. What?

BRINDSLEY. (*Frantically improvising.*) Dangerous! It's danger-

[69]

ous! . . . We can all die! Naked flames! Hideous accidents
can happen with naked flames!

HAROLD. I don't know what you're on about—what's up with
you?

(BRINDSLEY *clutches* HAROLD *and backs him bewilderedly
across to the center table.*)

BRINDSLEY. I've just remembered! It's something they always
warn you about. In old houses the fuse box and the gas
meter are in the same cupboard. They are here!

COLONEL. So what about it?

BRINDSLEY. Well . . . electrical blowouts can damage the gas
supply. They're famous for it. They do it all the time! And
they say you've got to avoid naked flames till they're mended.

COLONEL. I've never heard of that.

HAROLD. Me neither.

BRINDSLEY. Well, take my word for it. It's fantastically dangerous to burn a naked flame in this room!

CAROL. (*Catching on.*) Brin's absolutely right. In fact, they
warned me about it on the phone this evening when I called
them. They said, "Whatever you do, don't strike a match
till the fuse is mended."

BRINDSLEY. There, you see!—it's terribly dangerous.

COLONEL. (*Grimly.*) Then why didn't you warn me, Dumpling?

CAROL. I—I forgot.

COLONEL. Brilliant!

MISS FURNIVAL. Oh goodness, we must take care.

BRINDSLEY. We certainly must! . . . (*Pause.*) Let's all have a
drink. Cheer us up! . . .

CAROL. Good idea! Mr. Gorringe, would you like a drink?

HAROLD. Well, I must say, that wouldn't come amiss. Not after
the journey I've had tonight. I swear to God there was thirty-

five people in that compartment if there was one—babes in arms, toddlers, two nuns, three yapping poodles, and not a sausage to eat from Leamington to London. It's a bloody disgrace.

MISS FURNIVAL. You'd think they'd put on a restaurant car, Mr. Gorringe.

HAROLD. Not them, Ferny. They don't care if you perish once they've got your fare. Excuse me, I'll just go and clean up.

BRINDSLEY. (*Panic.*) You can do that here.

HAROLD. Well, I must unpack anyway.

BRINDSLEY. Do it later.

HAROLD. No, I hate to keep clothes in a suitcase longer than I absolutely have to. If there's one thing I can't stand, it's a creased suit.

BRINDSLEY. Five more minutes won't hurt, surely?

HAROLD. Ooh, you aren't half bossy!

CAROL. What will you have? Winnie, Vera or Ginette?

HAROLD. Come again?

CAROL. Winnie Whiskey, Vera Vodka, or dear old standby Ginette.

HAROLD. (*Yielding.*) I can see you're the camp one! . . . If it's all the same to you, I'll have a drop of Ginette, please, and a little lime juice.

COLONEL. Young man, do I have to keep reminding you that you are in an emergency? You have a guest arrivin' any second.

BRINDSLEY. Oh God, I'd forgotten!

COLONEL. Try the pub. Try the neighbors. Try who you damn well please, sir—but *get a torch!*

BRINDSLEY. Yes . . . Yes! . . . Carol, can I have a word with you, please?

CAROL. I'm here.

(SHE *gropes toward him and* BRINDSLEY *leads her to the stairs.*)

COLONEL. What now?

BRINDSLEY. Excuse us just a moment, please, Colonel.

(HE *pulls her quickly after him, up the stairs.*)

MISS FURNIVAL. (*As* THEY *do this.*) Oh, Mr. Gorringe, it's so exciting. You'll never guess who's coming here tonight.

HAROLD. Who?

MISS FURNIVAL. Guess.

HAROLD. The Queen!

MISS FURNIVAL. Oh, Mr. Gorringe, you are ridiculous!

(BRINDSLEY *arrives at the top of the stairs, then opens the bedroom door and closes it behind them.*)

BRINDSLEY. What are we going to do?

CAROL. (*Behind the door.*) I don't know!

BRINDSLEY. (*Behind the door.*) Think!

CAROL. But—

BRINDSLEY. *Think!*

COLONEL. Is that boy touched or somethin'?

HAROLD. Touched? He's an absolute poppet.

COLONEL. A what?

HAROLD. A duck. I've known him for years, ever since he came here. There's not many secrets we keep from each other, I can tell you.

COLONEL. (*Frostily.*) Really?

HAROLD. Yes, really. He's a very sweet boy.

(BRINDSLEY *and* CAROL *emerge from behind the bedroom door.*)

BRINDSLEY. We'll have to put all Harold's furniture back in his room.

CAROL. *Now?!*

BRINDSLEY. We'll have to. I can't get a torch till we do.

CAROL. We can't!

BRINDSLEY. We must. He'll go mad if he finds out what we've done.

HAROLD. Well come on, Ferny: don't be a tease. Who is it? Who's coming?

MISS FURNIVAL. I'll give you a clue. It's someone with money.

HAROLD. Money? . . . Let me think.

COLONEL. (*Calling out.*) Carol!

CAROL. Look, can't you just tell him it was a joke?

BRINDSLEY. You don't know him. He can't bear anyone to touch his treasures. They're like children to him. He cleans everything twice a day with a special swansdown duster. He'd wreck everything. Would you like him to call me a thief in front of your father?

CAROL. Of course not!

BRINDSLEY. Well, he would. He gets absolutely hysterical. I've seen him.

COLONEL. (*Mildly.*) Brindsley!

CAROL. Well, how the hell can we do it?

HAROLD. It's no good. You can't hear up there.

BRINDSLEY. (*Stripping off his jacket.*) Look, you hold the fort. Serve them drinks. Just keep things going. Leave it all to me. I'll try and put everything back in the dark.

CAROL. It won't work.

BRINDSLEY. It's *got* to!

COLONEL. (*Roaring.*) Brindsley!!

BRINDSLEY. (*Dashing to the door.*) Coming, sir . . . (*With false calm.*) I'm just getting some empties to take to the pub.

COLONEL. Say what you like. That boy's touched.

BRINDSLEY. (*To* CAROL, *intimately.*) Trust me, darling.

(THEY *kiss.*)

COLONEL. At the double, Miller.

BRINDSLEY. Yes, sir! Yes, sir!

(HE *rushes out and in his anxiety,* HE *misses his footing and falls neatly down the entire flight of stairs.*
Picking himself up.)

I'm off now, Colonel! Help is definitely on the way.

COLONEL. Well, hurry it up, man.

BRINDSLEY. Carol will give you drinks. If Mr. Bamberger arrives, just explain the situation to him.

HAROLD. (*Feeling for his hand.*) Would you like me to come with you?

BRINDSLEY. No, no, no—good heavens: stay and enjoy yourself.

(HAROLD *kisses his hand.* BRINDSLEY *pulls it away.*)

I mean, you must be exhausted after all those poodles. A nice gin and lime will do wonders. I shan't be a minute.

(HE *reaches the door, opens it, then slams it loudly, remaining on the inside. Stealthily* HE *opens it again, stands dead still for a moment, center, silently indicating to himself the position of the chairs* HE *has to move—then* HE *finds his way to the first of the Regency chairs, downstage left, which* HE *lifts noiselessly.*)

CAROL. (*With bright desperation.*) Well now, drinks! What's everyone going to have? It's Ginette for Mr. Gorringe and I suppose Winnie for Daddy.

COLONEL. And how on earth are you going to do that in the dark?

CAROL. I remember the exact way I put out the bottles.

(BRINDSLEY *bumps into her with the chair and falls back, gored by its leg.*)

CAROL. It's very simple.

HAROLD. Oh look, luv, let me strike a match. I'm sure it's not that dangerous, just for a minute. (HE *strikes a match.*)

CAROL. Oh no! . . .

(BRINDSLEY *ducks down, chair in hand, and blows out the match.*)

Do you want to blow us all up, Mr. Gorringe? . . . All poor Mr. Bamberger would find would be teensy weensy bits of us. Very messypegs.

(SHE *snatches the box of matches, feels for the ice bucket, and drops them into it.* BRINDSLEY *steals out, Felix-the-cat-like, with the chair as* CAROL *fumblingly starts to mix drinks.* HE *sets it down, opens* HAROLD'S *door, and disappears inside it with the chair.*)

HAROLD. Bamberger? Is that who's coming? Georg Bamberger?

MISS FURNIVAL. Yes. To see Mr. Miller's work. Isn't it exciting?

HAROLD. Well, I never. I read an article about him last week in the Sunday Pic. He's known as the mystery millionaire. He's almost completely deaf—deaf as a post, and spends most of his time indoors alone with his collection. He hardly ever goes out, except to a gallery or a private studio. That's the life! If I had money that's what I'd do. Just collect all the china and porcelain I wanted.

(BRINDSLEY *returns with a poor, broken-down chair of his own and sets it down in the same position as the one* HE *has taken out. The second chair presents a harder challenge. It sits right across the room, upstage right. Delicately* HE *moves towards it—but* HE *has difficulty finding it. We watch him walk round and round it in desperately narrowing circles till* HE *touches it and with relief picks it up.*)

MISS FURNIVAL. I've never met a millionaire. I've always wondered if they feel different to us. I mean their actual skins.

COLONEL. Their skins?

MISS FURNIVAL. Yes. I've always imagined they must be softer than ours. Like the skins of ladies when I was a girl.

[75]

CAROL. What an interesting idea.

HAROLD. Oh she's very fanciful is Ferny. Real imagination, I always say.

MISS FURNIVAL. Very kind of you, Mr. Gorringe. You're always so generous with your compliments.

(As SHE *speaks her next speech staring smugly into the darkness, hands clasped in maidenly gentility, the second Regency chair is being moved slowly across what should be her field of vision, two inches from her face. During the following,* BRINDSLEY *unfortunately misaims and carries the chair past the door, bumps into the wall, retreats from it, and inadvertently shuts the door softly with his back. Now* HE *cannot get out of the room.* HE *has to set down the chair, grope for the door handle, turn it, then open the door—then re-find the chair which* HE *has quite lost. This takes a long and frantic time. At last* HE *triumphs, and staggers from the room, nearly exhausted.*)

But this is by no means fancy. In my day, softness of skin was quite the sign of refinement. Nowadays, of course, it's hard enough for us middle classes to keep ourselves decently clothed, let alone soft. My father used to say, even before the bombs came and burnt our dear little house at Wendover: "The game's up, my girl. We middle classes are as dead as the dodo." Poor Father, how right he was.

————

NOTE: *Hopefully, if the counterpoint of farce action goes well,* MISS FURNIVAL *may have to ad-lib a fair bit during all this, and not mind too much if nobody hears her. The essential thing for all four actors during the furniture-moving is to preserve the look of ordinary conversation.*

COLONEL. Your father was a professional man?

MISS FURNIVAL. He was a man of God, Colonel.

COLONEL. Oh.

(BRINDSLEY *returns with a broken-down rocking chair of his own.* HE *crosses gingerly to where the* COLONEL *is sitting.*) How are those drinks coming, Dumpling?

CAROL. Fine, Daddy. They'll be one minute.

COLONEL. (*Speaking directly into* BRINDSLEY'S *face.*) Let me help you.

(BRINDSLEY *staggers back, startled.*)

CAROL. You can take this bitter lemon to Miss Furnival if you want.

(BRINDSLEY *sets down the rocker immediately next to the* COLONEL'S *chair.*)

COLONEL. Very well.

(HE *rises just as* BRINDSLEY'S *hand pulls it from beneath him. With his other hand* BRINDSLEY *pulls the rocker into the identical position. The* COLONEL *moves slowly across the room, arms outstretched for the bitter lemon. Unknowingly* BRINDSLEY *follows him, carrying the third chair. The* COLONEL *collides gently with the table. At the same moment* BRINDSLEY *reaches it upstage of him, and searches for the Wedgwood bowl. Their hands narrowly miss. Then the* YOUNG MAN *remembers the bowl is under the table. Deftly* HE *reaches down and retrieves it—and carrying it in one hand and the chair in the other, triumphantly leaves the room through the arch unconsciously provided by the outstretched arms of* CAROL *and the* COLONEL, *giving and receiving a glass of Scotch—which* THEY *think is lemonade.*)

CAROL. Here you are, Daddy. Bitter lemon for Miss Furnival.

COLONEL. Right you are, Dumpling. (*To* MISS FURNIVAL.) So your father was a minister then?

MISS FURNIVAL. He was a saint, Colonel. I'm only thankful he never lived to see the rudeness and vulgarity of life today.

(*The* COLONEL *sets off to find her but goes much too far to the right.*)

HAROLD. (HE *sits on the sofa beside her.*) Oooh, you're so right, Ferny. Rudeness and vulgarity—that's it to a T. The manners of some people today are beyond belief. Honestly. Did I tell you what happened in my shop last Friday? I don't think I did.

MISS FURNIVAL. No, Mr. Gorringe, I don't think so.

(*Her voice corrects the* COLONEL's *direction. During the following* HE *moves slowly up toward her.*)

HAROLD. Well, I'd just opened up—it was about quarter to ten and I was dusting off the teapots—you know, Rockingham collects the dust something shocking!—when who should walk in but that Mrs. Levitt, you know—the ginger-haired bit I told you about, the one who thinks she's God's gift to bachelors.

COLONEL. (*Finding her head with his hand and presenting her with the Scotch.*) Here's your lemonade.

MISS FURNIVAL. Oh, thank you. Most kind.

(*Throughout* HAROLD's *story,* MISS FURNIVAL *nurses the glass, not drinking. The* COLONEL *finds his way slowly back to the chair* HE *thinks* HE *was sitting on before, but which is now a rocker.* BRINDSLEY *re-appears triumphantly carrying one of the original Regency chairs* HE *took out.* HE *moves slowly across the room getting his bearings.*)

HAROLD. Anyway, she's got in her hand a vase I'd sold her last week—it was a birthday present for an old geezer she's having a bit of a ding dong with somewhere in Earls Court, hoping to collect all his lolly when he dies, as I read the situation. I'm a pretty good judge of character, Ferny, as you know—and she's a real grasper if ever I saw one.

(*The* COLONEL *sits heavily in the rocking chair which over-balances backward, spilling him onto the floor.*)

COLONEL. Dammit to hell!

CAROL. What's the matter, Daddy?

(*A pause.* BRINDSLEY *sits down panic-stricken on the chair* HE *has carried in. The* COLONEL *feels the chair and sets it on its feet.*)

COLONEL. (*Unbelieving.*) It's a blasted rockin' chair! I didn't see a blasted rockin' chair here before! . . .

(*Astounded, the* COLONEL *remains on the floor.* BRINDSLEY *rises and moves the chair to the original position of the second chair* HE *moved.*)

HAROLD. Oh yes, you want to watch that. It's in a pretty ropey condition, I've told Brin about it several times. Anyway, this vase. It's a nice bit of Kang Tsi, blue and white with a good orange-peel glaze, absolutely authentic—I'd let her have it for twenty-five pounds, and she'd got infinitely the best of the bargain, no argument about that.

(HAROLD *rises and leans against the center table to tell his story more effectively. The* COLONEL *seats himself again, gingerly.*)

Well, in she prances, her hair all done up in one of them bouffon hair-dos, you know, tarty—French-like—it would have looked fancy on a girl half her age with twice her looks—

(BRINDSLEY *mistakenly lifts the end of the sofa.* MISS FURNIVAL *gives a little scream at the jolt.*)

HAROLD. Exactly. You know the sort.

(BRINDSLEY *staggers in the opposite direction downstage onto the rostrum.*)

And d'you know what she says to me? "Mr. Gorringe," she says, "I've been cheated."

MISS FURNIVAL. No!

HAROLD. Her very words. "Cheated."

(BRINDSLEY *collides with the sculpture on the dais. It jangles violently.*

To it.)

Hush up, I'm talking!

CAROL. (*Covering up.*) I'm frightfully sorry.

(HAROLD *whirls round, surprised.*)

HAROLD. Anyway—"Oh, I say, and how exactly has that occurred, Mrs. Levitt?" "Well," she says, "quite by chance I took this vase over to Bill Everett in the Portobello, and he says it's not what you called it at all, Chinese and very rare. He says it's a piece of nineteenth-century English trash."

(BRINDSLEY *finds the lamp on the downstage table and picks it up.* HE *walks with it round the rocking chair, on which the* COLONEL *is now sitting again.*)

"Does he?" I say. "Does he?" I keep calm. I always do when I'm riled. "Yes," she says. "He does. And I'd thank you to give me money back."

(*The wire of the lamp has followed* BRINDSLEY *round the bottom of the rocking chair. It catches.* BRINDSLEY *tugs it gently. The chair moves. Surprised, the* COLONEL *jerks forward.* BRINDSLEY *tugs it again, much harder. The rocking chair is pulled forward, spilling the* COLONEL *out of it, again onto the floor, and then falling itself on top of him. The shade of the lamp comes off. During the ensuing dialogue* BRINDSLEY *gets to his knees and crawls right across the room following the flex of the lamp.* HE *finds the plug, pulls it out, and—still on his knees—re-traces his steps, winding up the wire around his arm, and becoming helplessly entangled in it. The* COLONEL *remains on the floor, now really alarmed.*)

MISS FURNIVAL. How dreadful, Mr. Gorringe. What did you do?

HAROLD. I counted to ten, and then I let her have it. "In the

first place," I said, "I don't expect my customers to go check-
ing up on my honesty behind my back. In the second, Bill
Everett is ignorant as Barnsley dirt, he doesn't know Tang
from Ting. And in the third place, that applies to you, too,
Mrs. Levitt."

MISS FURNIVAL. You didn't!

HAROLD. I certainly did—and worse than that. "You've got in
your hand," I said, "a minor masterpiece of Chinese pottery.
But in point of fact," I said, "you're not even fit to hold a
1953 Coronation mug. Don't you ever come in here again," I
said, "—don't you cross my threshold. Because if you do, Mrs.
Levitt, I won't make myself responsible for the conse-
quences."

CAROL. (*With two drinks in her hand.*) My, Mr. Gorringe, how
splendid of you. Here's your gin and lime. You deserve it.
(SHE *hands him the bitter lemon.*)

HAROLD. (*Accepting it.*) Ta. I was proper blazing, I didn't care.

CAROL. Where are you? Where are you, Daddy? Here's your
Scotch.

COLONEL. Here, Dumpling!
(HE *gets up dazedly and fumbles his way to the glass of gin
and lime.* BRINDSLEY *meanwhile realizes* HE *has lost the shade
of the lamp. On his knees,* HE *begins to look for it.*)

HAROLD. Carrotty old bitch—telling *me* about pottery! *Ooohl!*
(HE *shakes himself indignantly at the recollection of it.*)

MISS FURNIVAL. Do you care for porcelain yourself, Colonel?

COLONEL. I'm afraid I don't know very much about it, Madam.
I like some of that Chinese stuff—you get some lovely
colors, like on that statue I saw when I came in here—very
delicate.

HAROLD. What statue's that, Colonel?

COLONEL. The one on the packing case, sir. Very fine.

HAROLD. I didn't know Brin had any Chinese stuff. What's it of then, this statue?

(BRINDSLEY *freezes*.)

CAROL. (*Desperately*.) Well, we've all got drinks, I'd like to propose Daddy's regimental toast. Raise your glasses everyone! "To the dear old Twenty-Fifth Horse. Up the British, and Death to All Natives"!

MISS FURNIVAL. I'll drink to that!

HAROLD. Up the old Twenty-Fifth!!

(*Quickly* BRINDSLEY *finds the Buddha, moves it from the packing case to the table, then gets* HAROLD's *raincoat from the sofa, and wraps the statue up in it, leaving it on the table*.)

COLONEL. Thank you, Dumpling. That was very touchin' of you. Very touchin' indeed. (HE *swallows his drink*.) Dammit, that's gin!

HAROLD. I've got lemonade!

MISS FURNIVAL. Oh! Horrible! . . . Quite horrible! That would be alcohol, I suppose! . . . Oh dear, how unpleasant! . . .

HAROLD. (*To* MISS FURNIVAL.) Here, luv, exchange with me. No —you get the lemonade—but I get the gin. Colonel—

COLONEL. Here, sir.

(*Seizing her chance* MISS FURNIVAL *downs a huge draft of Scotch.* THEY *all exchange drinks.* BRINDSLEY *resumes his frantic search for the shade.*)

HAROLD. Here, Ferny.

(*The* COLONEL *hands her the gin and lime.* HE *gets instead the bitter lemon from* HAROLD. HAROLD *gets the Scotch.*)

MISS FURNIVAL. Thank you.

HAROLD. Well, let's try again. Bottoms up!

COLONEL. Quite.

(THEY *drink. Triumphantly,* BRINDSLEY *finds the shade. Un-*

fortunately at the same moment the COLONEL *spits out his lemonade in a fury all over him, as he marches toward him on his knees.*)

Look here—I can't stand another minute of this!

(HE *fishes his lighter out of his pocket and angrily tries to light it.*)

CAROL. Daddy, please!

COLONEL. I don't care, Dumpling. If I blow us up, then I'll blow us up! This is ridiculous . . .

(*His words die in the flame.* HE *spies* BRINDSLEY *kneeling at his feet, wound about with lampwire.*)

What the devil are you doin' there?

BRINDSLEY. (*Blowing out his lighter.*) Now don't be rash, Colonel! Isn't the first rule of an officer "Don't involve your men in unnecessary danger"?

(*Quickly* HE *steals, still on his knees, to the table downstage right.*)

COLONEL. Don't be impertinent. Where's the torch?

BRINDSLEY. Er . . . the pub was closed.

HAROLD. You didn't go to the pub in that time, surely? You couldn't have done.

BRINDSLEY. Of course I did.

MISS FURNIVAL. But it's five streets away, Mr. Miller.

BRINDSLEY. Needs must when the devil drives, Miss Furnival. Whatever that means.

(*Quickly* HE *lifts the table, and steals out of the room with it and the wrecked lamp.*)

COLONEL. (*Who thinks* HE *is still kneeling at his feet.*) Now look here: there's somethin' very peculiar goin' on in this room. I may not know about art, Miller, but I know men. I know a liar in the light, and I know one in the dark.

CAROL. Daddy!

[83]

COLONEL. I don't want to doubt your word, sir. All the same, I'd like your oath you went out to that public house. *Well?*

CAROL. (*Realizing* HE *isn't there, raising her voice.*) Brin, Daddy's talking to you!

COLONEL. What are you shoutin' for?

BRINDSLEY. (*Rushing back from* HAROLD's *room, still entangled in the lamp.*) Of course. I know. He's absolutely right. I was—just thinking it over for a moment.

COLONEL. Well? What's your answer?

BRINDSLEY. I . . . I couldn't agree with you more, sir.

COLONEL. What?

BRINDSLEY. That was a very perceptive remark you made there. Not everyone would have thought of that. Individual. You know. Almost witty. Well, it *was* witty. Why be ungenerous? . . .

COLONEL. Look, young man, are you trying to be funny?

BRINDSLEY. (*Ingratiatingly.*) Well, I'll try anything once . . .

HAROLD. I say, this is becoming a bit unpleasant, isn't it?

CAROL. It's becoming drearypegs.

COLONEL. Quiet, Dumpling. Let me handle this.

BRINDSLEY. What's there to handle, sir?

COLONEL. If you think I'm going to let my daughter marry a born liar, you're very much mistaken.

HAROLD. Marry!

CAROL. Well, that's the idea.

HAROLD. You and this young lady, Brin?

CAROL. Are what's laughingly known as engaged. Subject of course to Daddy's approval.

HAROLD. Well! (*Furious at the news, and at the fact that* BRINDSLEY *hasn't confided in him.*) What a surprise! . . .

BRINDSLEY. We were keeping it a secret.

HAROLD. Evidently. How long's this been going on, then?

BRINDSLEY. A few months.

HAROLD. You old slyboots.

BRINDSLEY. (*Nervous.*) I hope you approve, Harold.

HAROLD. Well, I must say, you know how to keep things to yourself.

BRINDSLEY. (*Placatingly.*) I meant to tell you, Harold . . . I really did. You were the one person I was going to tell.

HAROLD. Well why didn't you, then?

BRINDSLEY. I don't know. I just never got around to it.

HAROLD. You saw me every day.

BRINDSLEY. I know.

HAROLD. You could have mentioned it at any time.

BRINDSLEY. I know.

HAROLD. (*Huffy.*) Well, it's your business. There's no obligation to share confidences. I've only been your neighbor for three years. I've always assumed there was more than a geographical closeness between us, but I was obviously mistaken.

BRINDSLEY. Oh don't start getting huffy, Harold.

HAROLD. I'm not getting anything. I'm just saying it's surprising, that's all. Surprising and somewhat disappointing.

BRINDSLEY. Oh look, Harold, please understand—

HAROLD. (*Shrill.*) There's no need to say anything! It'll just teach me in future not to bank too much on friendship. It's silly me again! Silly, stupid, trusting me!

(MISS FURNIVAL *rises in agitation and gropes her way to the drinks table.*)

COLONEL. Good God!

CAROL. (*Wheedling.*) Oh come, Mr. Gorringe. We haven't told anybody. Not one single soulipegs. Really.

COLONEL. At the moment, Dumpling, there's nothing to tell. And I'm not sure there's going to be!

BRINDSLEY. Look, sir, we seem to have got off on the wrong foot. If it's my fault, I apologize.

MISS FURNIVAL. (*Groping about on the drinks table.*) My father always used to say, "To err is human: to forgive divine."

CAROL. I thought that was somebody else.

MISS FURNIVAL. (*Blithely.*) So many people copied him. (SHE *finds the open bottle of gin, lifts it and sniffs it eagerly.*)

CAROL. May I help you, Miss Furnival?

MISS FURNIVAL. No, thank you, Miss Melkett. I'm just getting myself another bitter lemon. That is—if I may, Mr. Miller?

BRINDSLEY. Of course. Help yourself.

MISS FURNIVAL. Thank you, most kind!

(SHE *pours more gin into her glass and returns slowly to sit upstage on the edge of the rostrum.*)

COLONEL. Well, sir, wherever you are—

BRINDSLEY. Here, Colonel.

COLONEL. I'll overlook your damn peculiar behavior this once, but understand this, Miller. My daughter's dear to me. You show me you can look after her, and I'll consider the whole thing most favorably. I can't say fairer than that, can I?

BRINDSLEY. No, sir. Most fair, sir. Most fair. (HE *pulls a hideous face one inch from the* COLONEL'S.)

CAROL. Of course he can look after me, Daddy. His works are going to be world-famous. In five years I'll feel just like Mrs. Michaelangelo.

HAROLD. (*Loftily.*) There wasn't a Mrs. Michaelangelo, actually.

CAROL. (*Irritated.*) Wasn't there?

HAROLD. No. He had passionate feelings of a rather different nature.

CAROL. Really, Mr. Gorringe. I didn't know that. (SHE *puts out her tongue at him.*)

BRINDSLEY. Look, Harold, I'm sorry if I've hurt your feelings.

[86]

HAROLD. (*Loftily.*) You haven't.

BRINDSLEY. I know I have. Please forgive me.

CAROL. Oh, do, Mr. Gorringe. Quarreling is so dreary. I hope we're all going to be great friends.

HAROLD. I'm not sure that I can contemplate a friendly relationship with a viper.

MISS FURNIVAL. Remember: to err is human, to forgive divine!

COLONEL. (*Irritated.*) You just said that, madam.

(CLEA *enters, wearing dark glasses and carrying an air-bag.* SHE *stands in the doorway, amazed by the dark.* SHE *takes off her glasses, but this doesn't improve matters.*)

MISS FURNIVAL. (*Downing her gin happily.*) Did I?

CAROL. Brin's not really a viper. He's just artistic, aren't you, darling?

BRINDSLEY. Yes, darling.

(CAROL *sends him an audible kiss across the astonished* CLEA. HE *returns it, equally audibly.*)

CAROL. (*Winningly.*) Come on, Mr. Gorringe. It really is a case of forgive and forgettipegs.

HAROLD. Is it reallypegs?

CAROL. Have another Ginette and lime. I'll have one with you.

(SHE *rises and mixes the drink.*)

HAROLD. (*Rising.*) Oh, all right. I don't mind if I do.

CAROL. Let me mix it for you.

HAROLD. Ta.

(HE *crosses to her, narrowly missing* CLEA *who is now crossing the room to the sofa, and gets his drink.*)

I must say there's nothing nicer than having a booze up with a pretty girl.

CAROL. (*Archly.*) You haven't seen me yet.

HAROLD. Oh, I just know it. Brindsley always had wonderful

[87]

taste. I've often said to him, you've got the same taste in ladies as I have in porcelain. Ta.

(HAROLD *and* BRINDSLEY—*one from upstage, one from across the room—begin to converge on the sofa. On the word "modest"* ALL THREE, CLEA *in the middle, sit on it.* BRINDSLEY *of course imagines* HE *is sitting next to* HAROLD.)

BRINDSLEY. Harold!

CAROL. Oh don't be silly, Brin. Why be so modest? I found a photograph of one of his bits from two years ago, and I must say she was pretty stunning in a blowsy sort of way.

HAROLD. Which one was that, then? I suppose she means Clea.

CAROL. Did you know her, Mr. Gorringe?

HAROLD. Oh yes. She's been around a long time.

(BRINDSLEY *nudges* CLEA *warningly—imagining* SHE *is* HAROLD. CLEA *gently bumps* HAROLD.)

CAROL. (*Surprised.*) Has she?

HAROLD. Oh yes, dear. Or am I speaking out of turn?

BRINDSLEY. Not at all. I've told Carol all about Clea. (HE *bangs* CLEA *again, a little harder—who correspondingly bumps against* HAROLD.) Though I must say, Harold, I'm surprised you call three months "a long time."

(CLEA *shoots him a look of total outrage at this lie.* HAROLD *is also astonished.*)

CAROL. What was she like?

BRINDSLEY. (*Meaningfully, into* CLEA'S *ear.*) I suppose you can hardly remember her, Harold.

HAROLD. (*Speaking across her.*) Why on earth shouldn't I?

BRINDSLEY. Well, since it was two years ago, you've probably forgotten.

HAROLD. Two years?!

BRINDSLEY. *Two years ago!*

(HE *punches* CLEA *so hard that the rebound knocks* HAROLD *off the sofa, drink and all.*)

[88]

HAROLD. (*Picking himself up. Spitefully.*) Well, now since you mention it, I remember her perfectly. I mean, she's not one you can easily forget!

CAROL. Was she pretty?

HAROLD. No, not at all. In fact, I'd say the opposite. Actually she was rather plain.

BRINDSLEY. She wasn't!

HAROLD. I'm just giving my opinion.

BRINDSLEY. You've never given it before.

HAROLD. (*Leaning over* CLEA.) I was never asked! But since it's come up, I always thought she was ugly. For one thing, she had teeth like a picket fence—yellow and spiky. And for another, she had bad skin.

BRINDSLEY. She had nothing of the kind!

HAROLD. She did. I remember it perfectly. It was like new pink wallpaper, with an old gray crumbly paper underneath.

MISS FURNIVAL. Quite right, Mr. Gorringe. I hardly ever saw her, but I do recall her skin. It was a strange color, as you say —and very coarse . . . Not soft, as the skins of young ladies should be, if they *are* young ladies.

(CLEA *rises in outrage.*)

HAROLD. Aye, that's right. Coarse.

MISS FURNIVAL. And rather lumpy.

HAROLD. Very lumpy.

BRINDSLEY. This is disgraceful.

HAROLD. You knew I never liked her, Brindsley. She was too clever by half.

MISS FURNIVAL. And so tiresomely Bohemian.

CAROL. You mean she was as pretentious as her name?

(CLEA, *who has been reacting to this last exchange of comments about her like a spectator at a tennis match, now reacts to* CAROL *open-mouthed.*)

I bet she was. That photograph I found showed her in a

dirndl and a sort of sultry peasant blouse. She looked like "The Bartered Bride" done by Lloyds Bank.

(THEY *laugh,* BRINDSLEY *hardest of all. Guided by the noise,* CLEA *aims her hand and slaps his face.*)

BRINDSLEY. Ahh!

CAROL. What's wrong?

MISS FURNIVAL. What is it, Mr. Miller?

BRINDSLEY. (*Furious.*) That's not very funny, Harold. What the hell's the matter with you?

(CLEA *makes her escape.*)

HAROLD. (*Indignant.*) With me?

BRINDSLEY. Well, I'm sure it wasn't the Colonel.

COLONEL. What wasn't, sir?

(BRINDSLEY, *groping about, catches* CLEA *by the bottom, and instantly recognizes it.*)

BRINDSLEY. Clea! . . . (*In horror.*) Clea!!

(CLEA *breaks loose and moves away from him. During the following* HE *tries to find her in the dark, and* SHE *narrowly avoids him.*)

COLONEL. What?

BRINDSLEY. I was just remembering her, sir. You're all talking the most awful nonsense. She was beautiful . . . And anyway, Harold, you just said I was famous for my taste in women.

HAROLD. Aye, but it had its lapses.

BRINDSLEY. (*Frantically moving about.*) Rubbish! She was beautiful and tender and considerate and kind and loyal and witty and adorable in every way!

CAROL. You told me she was as cozy as a steel razor blade.

BRINDSLEY. Did I? Surely not! No. What I said was . . . something quite different . . . Utterly different . . . entirely different . . . As different as chalk from cheese. Although when you come to think of it, cheese isn't all that different from chalk. (HE *gives his braying laugh.*)

COLONEL. Are you sure you know what you're talking about?

(*During this* CLEA *has reached the table, picked up a bottle of Scotch, and rejected it in favor of vodka, which* SHE *takes with her.*)

CAROL. You said to me in this room when I asked you what she was like, "She was a painter. Very honest. Very clever, and just about as cozy—"

BRINDSLEY. (*Stopping, exasperated.*) As a steel razor blade! Well then, I said it! So bloody what? . . .

CAROL. So nothing!

(HE *throws out his hands in a gesture of desperate exhaustion and bumps straight into* CLEA. THEY *instantly embrace,* CLEA *twining herself around him, her vodka bottle held aloft. A tiny pause.*)

COLONEL. If that boy isn't touched, I don't know the meaning of the word!

CAROL. What's all this talk about her being kind and tender, all of a sudden?

BRINDSLEY. (*Tenderly, holding* CLEA.) She could be. On occasion. Very.

CAROL. Very rare occasions, I imagine.

BRINDSLEY. Not so rare. (HE *kisses* CLEA *again.*) Not so rare at all. (HE *leads her softly past the irritated* CAROL, *toward the stairs.*)

CAROL. Meaning what, exactly? . . . (*Shouting.*) Brindsley, I'm talking to you!

BRINDSLEY. (*Sotto voce, into* CLEA's *ear as* THEY *stand just behind* HAROLD.) I can explain. Go up to the bedroom. Wait for me there.

[91]

HAROLD. (*In amazement: thinking* HE *is being addressed.*) Now? Do you think this is quite the moment?

BRINDSLEY. Oh God! . . . I wasn't talking to you.

CAROL. What did you say?

HAROLD. (*To* CAROL.) I think he wants *you* upstairs. (*Slyly.*) For what purpose, I can't begin to imagine.

COLONEL. They're going to do some more of that plotting, I daresay.

MISS FURNIVAL. Lover's talk, Colonel.

COLONEL. Very touching, I'm sure.

(BRINDSLEY *pushes* CLEA *ahead of him up the stairs.*)

MISS FURNIVAL. "Journeys end in lovers meeting," as my father always used to say.

COLONEL. What a strikingly original father you seem to have had, madam.

(CAROL *joins the* OTHER TWO *on the stairs. We see* ALL THREE *groping blindly up to the bedroom,* BRINDSLEY'S *hands on* CLEA'S *hips,* CAROL'S *on* BRINDSLEY'S.)

CAROL. (*With a conspirator's stage whisper.*) What is it, darling? Has something gone wrong? What can't you move? (*This next dialogue sotto voce.*)

BRINDSLEY. Nothing. It's all back—every bit of it—except the sofa, and I've covered that up.

CAROL. You mean, we can have lights?

BRINDSLEY. Yes . . . NO!!

CAROL. Why not?

BRINDSLEY. Never mind!

CAROL. Why do you want me in the bedroom?

BRINDSLEY. I don't. Go away!

CAROL. Charming!

BRINDSLEY. I didn't mean that.

COLONEL. There you are. They *are* plotting again. What the hell is going on up there?

BRINDSLEY. Nothing, Colonel. I've just remembered—there may be a torch under my bed. I keep it to blind the burglars with. Have another drink, Colonel!

(HE *pushes* CLEA *into the bedroom and shuts the door.*)

COLONEL. What d'you mean another? I haven't had one yet.

MISS FURNIVAL. Oh! Poor Colonel! Let me get you one.

COLONEL. (*Rising.*) I can get one for myself, thank you. Let me get you another lemonade.

MISS FURNIVAL. (*Rising.*) No thank you, Colonel, I'll manage myself. It's good practice!

(THEY *grope toward the drinks table. Above,* CLEA *and* BRINDSLEY *sit on the bed.*)

CLEA. So this is what they mean by a blind date. What the hell is going on?

BRINDSLEY. (*Sarcastic.*) Nothing! Georg Bamberger is only coming to see my work tonight, and we've got a main fuse.

CLEA. Is that the reason for all this furtive clutching?

BRINDSLEY. Look, I can't explain things at the moment.

CLEA. Who's that—(*Debutante accent*) "frightful gel"?

BRINDSLEY. Just a friend.

CLEA. She sounded more than that.

BRINDSLEY. Well, if you must know, it's Carol. I've told you about her.

CLEA. The Idiot Deb?

BRINDSLEY. She's a very sweet girl. As a matter of fact we've become very good friends in the last six weeks.

CLEA. How good?

BRINDSLEY. Just good.

CLEA. And have you become friends with her father too?

BRINDSLEY. If it's any of your business, they just dropped in to meet Mr. Bamberger.

CLEA. What was it you wanted to tell me on the phone to-night?

BRINDSLEY. Nothing.

CLEA. You're lying!

BRINDSLEY. Ah, here comes the inquisition! Look, Clea, if you ever loved me, just slip away quietly with no more questions, and I'll come round later and explain everything, I promise.

CLEA. I don't believe you.

BRINDSLEY. Please darling . . . Please . . . Please . . . Please!!

(THEY *kiss, passionately, stretched out on the bed.*)

COLONEL. (*Pouring.*) At last . . . a decent glass of Scotch. Are you getting your lemonade?

MISS FURNIVAL. (*Cheerfully pouring herself an enormous gin.*) Oh yes, thank you, Colonel!

COLONEL. I'm just wonderin' if this Bamberger fellow is goin' to show up at all. He's half an hour late already.

HAROLD. Oh! That's nothing, Colonel. Millionaires are always late. It's their thing.

MISS FURNIVAL. I'm sure you're right, Mr. Gorringe. That's how *I* imagine them. Hands like silk, and always two hours late.

CAROL. Brin's been up there a long time. What can he be doing?

HAROLD. Maybe he's got that Clea hidden away in his bed-room, and they're having a tête-à-tête!!

CAROL. What a flagrant suggestion, Mr. Gorringe.

BRINDSLEY. (*Disengaging himself.*) No one in the world kisses like you.

CLEA. I missed you so badly, Brin. I had to see you. I've thought about nothing else these past six weeks. Brin, I made the most awful mistake walking out.

BRINDSLEY. Clea—*please!*

CLEA. I mean we've known each other for four years. We can't just throw each other away like old newspapers.

BRINDSLEY. I don't see why not. You know my politics, you've heard my gossip, and you've certainly been through all my entertainment section.

CLEA. Well, how about a second edition?

BRINDSLEY. Darling, we simply can't talk about this now. Can't you trust me just for an hour?

CLEA. Of course I can, darling. You don't want me down there?

BRINDSLEY. No.

CLEA. Then I'll get undressed and go quietly to bed. When you've got rid of them all, I'll be waiting.

BRINDSLEY. That's a terrible idea!

CLEA. (*Reaching for him.*) I think it's lovely. A little happy relaxation for us both.

BRINDSLEY. (*Falling off the bed.*) I'm perfectly relaxed!

CAROL. Brindsley!

CLEA. "Too solemn for day, too sweet for night. Come not in darkness, come not in light." That's me, isn't it?

BRINDSLEY. Of course not. I just can't explain now, that's all.

CLEA. Oh, very well, you can explain later . . . in bed!

BRINDSLEY. Not tonight, Clea.

CLEA. Either that or I come down and discover your sordid secret.

BRINDSLEY. There *is* no sordid secret!

CLEA. Then you won't mind my coming down!

CAROL, COLONEL. (*Roaring together.*) BRINDSLEY!!!

BRINDSLEY. Oh God!! . . . All right, stay. Only keep quiet . . . Blackmailing bitch! (HE *emerges at the top of the stairs.*) Yes, my sweet?

CAROL. What are you doing up there? You've been an eternity!

BRINDSLEY. I . . . I . . . I'm just looking in the bathroom, my darling. You never know what you might find in that clever little cabinet.

COLONEL. (*Moving to the stairs.*) Are you trying to madden me, sir? Are you trying to put me in a fury?

BRINDSLEY. Certainly not, sir!!

COLONEL. I warn you, Miller, it's not difficult! In the old days in the regiment I was known for my furies. I was famous for my furies . . . Do you hear?

CLEA. I may sing!

(SHE *goes off into the bathroom.*)

BRINDSLEY. I may knock your teeth in!

COLONEL. What did you say?

CAROL. Brin! How dare you talk to Daddy like that!

BRINDSLEY. Oh!! I . . . I . . . I wasn't talking to Daddy like that . . .

CAROL. Then who *were* you talking to?

BRINDSLEY. I was talking to no one! Myself I was talking to! I was saying . . . "If I keep groping about up here like this, I might knock my teeth in!"

COLONEL. Mad! . . . Mad! . . . Mad as the south wind! It's the only explanation—you've got yourself engaged to a lunatic.

CAROL. There's something going on up there, and I'm coming up to find out what it is. Do you hear me, Brin?

BRINDSLEY. Carol—no!

CAROL. (*Climbing the stairs.*) I'm not such a fool as you take me for. I know when you're hiding something. Your voice goes all deceitful—very, very foxipegs!

BRINDSLEY. Darling please. That's not very ladylike . . . I'm sure the Colonel won't approve of you entering a man's bedroom in the dark!

(*Enter* SCHUPPANZIGH. HE *wears the overcoat and peaked cap*

*of the London Electricity Board and carries a large tool bag,
similarly labeled.)*

CAROL. I'm comin' up, Brindsley, I'm comin' up!!!

BRINDSLEY. (*Scrambling down.*) I'm coming down . . . We'll
all have a nice cozy drink . . .

SCHUPPANZIGH. 'Allo please? Mr. Miller? Mr. Miller? I've come
as was arranged.

BRINDSLEY. My God . . . it's Bamberger!

CAROL. Bamberger?

BRINDSLEY. Yes, Bamberger. (BRINDSLEY *rushes down the remaining stairs, pulling* CAROL *with him.*)

SCHUPPANZIGH. You must have thought I was never coming!
(HE *takes off his overcoat and cap.*)

BRINDSLEY. Not at all. I'm delighted you could spare the time.
I know how busy you are. I'm afraid we've had the most
idiotic disaster. We've had a fuse.

HAROLD. You'll have to speak up, dear. He's stone deaf!

BRINDSLEY. (*Yelling.*) We've had a fuse—not the best condi-
tions for seeing sculpture.

SCHUPPANZIGH. Please not to worry. Here!

(HE *produces a torch from his pocket and "lights" it. The
light on stage dims a little, as usual, to indicate this.*
ALL *relax with audible sighs of pleasure.*

SCHUPPANZIGH *at once places his tool bag on the Regency
chair, and puts his coat and cap on top of it, concealing that
it is one of* HAROLD's *chairs.*)

CAROL. Oh what a relief!

BRINDSLEY. (*Hastily dragging the sheet over the rest of the
sofa.*) Do you always travel with a torch?

SCHUPPANZIGH. Mostly, yes. It helps to see details. (*Seeing the
OTHERS.*) You are holding a private view?

[97]

MISS FURNIVAL. Oh no! I was just going. I'd hate to distract you.

SCHUPPANZIGH. Please not on my account, dear lady. I am not so easily distracted.

MISS FURNIVAL. (*Charmed.*) Oh! . . .

BRINDSLEY. (*Yelling in his ear.*) May I present Colonel Melkett?

COLONEL. (*Yelling in his other ear.*) A great honor, sir!

SCHUPPANZIGH. (*Banging his ear, to clear it.*) No, no, mine—mine!

BRINDSLEY. Miss Carol Melkett.

CAROL. (*Screeching in his ear.*) I say: hello. So glad you got here! It's terribly kind of you to take such an interest!

SCHUPPANZIGH. Not at all. *Vous êtes très gentil.*

CAROL. (*Yelling.*) What would you like to drink?

SCHUPPANZIGH. (*Bewildered.*) A little vodka, would be beautiful!

CAROL. Of course!

BRINDSLEY. Harold Gorringe—a neighbor of mine!

HAROLD. How do? Very honored, I'm sure.

SCHUPPANZIGH. Enchanted.

HAROLD. I must say it's a real thrill, meeting you!

BRINDSLEY. And another neighbor, Miss Furnival.

SCHUPPANZIGH. Enchanted.

MISS FURNIVAL. (*Hooting in his ear.*) I'm afraid we've all been taking refuge from the *storm*, as it were. (*Exclaiming as* SHE *holds* SCHUPPANZIGH's *hand.*) Oh! It *is* true! They *are* softer! Much, much softer!

SCHUPPANZIGH. (*Utterly confused as* SHE *strokes his hand.*) Softer? Please?

(BRINDSLEY *and* HAROLD *pull her away, and* SHE *subsides onto the sofa.*)

BRINDSLEY. Miss Furnival, please!

CAROL. (*At the drinks table.*) Darling, where's the vodka?

BRINDSLEY. It's on the table.

CAROL. No, it isn't.

BRINDSLEY. It must be!

(*Above,* CLEA *re-enters wearing the top half of* BRINDSLEY's *pajamas and nothing else.* SHE *gets into bed, still clutching the vodka bottle and carrying a plastic toothmug.*)

CAROL. Well, see for yourself. There's Winnie and Ginette, and Vera has quite vanished, the naughty girl.

BRINDSLEY. She can't have done.

SCHUPPANZIGH. Please don't concern yourselves. I am pressed for time. If I might just be shown where to go.

BRINDSLEY. Of course. It's through the studio there. Darling, if you would just show our guest into the studio—*with his torch.*

CAROL. What?? . . .

BRINDSLEY. (*Sotto voce.*) *The sofa!* . . . Get him out of here.

CAROL. Oh yes!!

SCHUPPANZIGH. (*Sighting the sculpture.*) Oh! Good gracious! What an extraordinary object!

BRINDSLEY. Oh, that's just a spare piece of my work I keep in here!

SCHUPPANZIGH. Spare, maybe, but fascinating!

BRINDSLEY. You really think so?

SCHUPPANZIGH. (*Approaching it.*) I do! Ja!

BRINDSLEY. Well, in that case you should see my main collection. It's next door. My fiancée will show you!

(MISS FURNIVAL *sits on the sofa.* SHE *is now quite drunk.*)

SCHUPPANZIGH. One amazement at a time, if you please! In this gluttonous age it is easy to get visual indigestion—hard to find visual Alka Seltzer . . . Permit me to digest this first!

BRINDSLEY. Oh, by all means . . . Good, yes . . . There's no hurry—no hurry at all . . . Only . . . (*Inspired.*) Why don't you digest it *in the dark?*

SCHUPPANZIGH. I beg your pardon?

BRINDSLEY. You'll never believe it, sir, but I actually made that piece to be appreciated in the dark. I was working on a very interesting theory. You know how the Victorians said, "Children should be seen and not heard"? Well, I say, "Art should be felt and not seen."

SCHUPPANZIGH. Amazing.

BRINDSLEY. Yes, isn't it. I call it my theory of Factual Tactility. If it doesn't stab you to the quick—it's not art. Look! Why don't you give me that torch, and try for yourself?

SCHUPPANZIGH. Very well, I will!! (HE *hands* BRINDSLEY *the torch.*)

BRINDSLEY. Thank you!

(HE *turns off the torch and hands it to* CAROL. *At the same moment* MISS FURNIVAL *quietly lies down, her full length on the sofa.*)

Now just stretch out your arms and feel it all over, sir.

(HE *steals toward the studio.*)

Have a good long feel!

(SCHUPPANZIGH *embraces the metal sculpture with a fervent clash.* HE *pulls at the two metal prongs.*)

Do you see what I mean?

(*Silently* HE *opens the curtains.*)

SCHUPPANZIGH. Amazing! . . . Absolutely incredible! . . . It's quite true . . . Like this, the piece becomes a masterpiece at once.

BRINDSLEY. (*Astonished.*) It does??

SCHUPPANZIGH. But of course! I feel it here—and here—the two needles of man's unrest! . . . Self love and self hate, leading to the same point! That's the meaning of the work, isn't it?

BRINDSLEY. Of course. You've got it in one! You're obviously a great expert, sir!

(*Quietly* HE *pulls the sofa into the studio, bearing on it the supine* MISS FURNIVAL, *who waves good-bye as she disappears.*)

SCHUPPANZIGH. Not at all. V*ous êtes très gentil*—but it is evident . . . Standing here in the dark, one can feel the vital thrust of the argument! The essential anguish! The stress and the torment of our times! It is simple but not simpleminded! Ingenious, but not ingenuous! Above all, it has real moral force! Of how many modern works can one say that, good people?

CAROL. Oh, none, none at all really.

SCHUPPANZIGH. I hope I do not lecture. It can be a fault with me.

CAROL. Not at all! I could listen all night, it's so profound.

HAROLD. Me too. Really deep!

COLONEL. I don't know anything about this myself, sir, but it's an honor to listen to you.

(HE *starts off upstage in search of the sofa, seating himself tentatively in the air, then moving himself along in a sitting position, trying to find it with his rear end.*

At the same moment BRINDSLEY *emerges from the studio, closes the curtains behind him, and gropes his way to the upstage corner where there stands a small packing-case. This he carries forward, hopefully to do duty for the missing sofa. Just as* HE *places it on the ground the traveling* COLONEL *sits on it, trapping* BRINDSLEY's *hand beneath his weight. During the following,* BRINDSLEY *tries frantically to free himself.*)

SCHUPPANZIGH. *Vous êtes très gentil!*

HAROLD. You mean to say you see all that in a bit of metal?

SCHUPPANZIGH. A *tiny* bit of metal, that's the point. A miracle of compression! You want my opinion, this boy is a genius. A master of the miniature. In the space of a matchbox he can realize anything he wants—the black virginity of Chartres! The white chorale of the Acropolis! *Wunderbar!*

CAROL. Oh how super!

SCHUPPANZIGH. You should charge immense sums for work like this, Mr. Miller. They should be very very expensive! This one, for example, how much is this?

BRINDSLEY. Fifty.

CAROL. Five hundred guineas.

SCHUPPANZIGH. Ah so! Very cheap.

HAROLD. Cheap!

CAROL. I think so, Mr. Gorringe. Well . . . so will you have it then?

SCHUPPANZIGH. Me?

BRINDSLEY. Darling . . . aren't you rushing things just a little? Perhaps you would like to see the rest of my work.

SCHUPPANZIGH. Alas, I have no more time. To linger would be pleasant, but alas, I must work . . . Also, as Moses discovered, it is sufficient to glimpse milk and honey. One does not have to wolf them down!

BRINDSLEY. Well.

COLONEL. Well . . .

HAROLD. Well. . . .

CAROL. Well . . . Would you like it then?

SCHUPPANZIGH. Very much.

COLONEL. (*Rising.* BRINDSLEY *is freed at last.*) For five hundred guineas?

SCHUPPANZIGH. Certainly—if I had it!

HAROLD. According to the Sunday Pictorial, you must be worth at least seventeen million pounds.

SCHUPPANZIGH. The Sunday papers are notoriously ill-informed. According to my bank statement, I was worth one hundred pounds, eight shillings and fourpence.

HAROLD. You mean you've gone broke?

SCHUPPANZIGH. No. I mean I never had any more.

COLONEL. Now look, sir, I know millionaires are supposed to be eccentric, but this is gettin' tiresome.

CAROL. Daddy, ssh!—

SCHUPPANZIGH. Millionaires? Who do you think I am?

COLONEL. Dammit, man!—You must know who you are!

CAROL. Mr. Bamberger, is this some kind of joke you like to play?

SCHUPPANZIGH. Excuse me. That is not my name.

BRINDSLEY. It isn't?

SCHUPPANZIGH. No. My name is Schuppanzigh. Franz Schuppanzigh. Born in Weimar 1905. Student of Philosophy at Heidelberg 1934. Refugee to this country, 1938. Regular employment ever since with the London Electricity Board.

(ALL *rise*.)

CAROL. Electricity?

MISS FURNIVAL. Electricity!

BRINDSLEY. You mean you're not?—

HAROLD. Of course he's not!

SCHUPPANZIGH. But who did you imagine I was?

HAROLD. (*Furious.*) How dare you? (HE *snatches the* ELECTRICIAN's *torch.*)

SCHUPPANZIGH. (*Retreating before him.*) Please?—

HAROLD. Of all the nerve, coming in here, giving us a lecture about needles and virgins, and all the time you're simply here to mend the fuses!

[103]

COLONEL. I agree with you, sir. It's monstrous!

SCHUPPANZIGH. (*Bewildered.*) It is?

(*The* COLONEL *takes the torch and shines it pitilessly in the* MAN'*s face.*)

COLONEL. You come in here, a public servant, and proceed to harangue your employers, unasked and uninvited.

SCHUPPANZIGH. (*Bewildered.*) Excuse me. But I *was* invited.

COLONEL. Don't answer back. In my day you would have been fired on the spot for impertinence.

CAROL. Daddy's absolutely right! Ever since the Beatles, the lower classes think they can behave exactly as they want.

COLONEL. (*Handing the torch to* BRINDSLEY.) Miller, will you kindly show this feller his work?

BRINDSLEY. The mains are in the cellar. There's a trapdoor. (*Indicating.*) Do you mind?

SCHUPPANZIGH. (*Snatching the torch furiously.*) Why should I mind? It's why I came, after all! (HE *takes his coat, cap, and bag off* HAROLD'*s Regency chair . . . Seeing it.*) Now there is a really beautiful chair!

(BRINDSLEY *stares at the chair aghast—and in a twinkling seats himself in it to conceal it.*)

BRINDSLEY. (*Exasperated.*) Why don't you just go into the cellar?

SCHUPPANZIGH. *How? Where is it?*

BRINDSLEY. (*To* CAROL.) Darling, will you open the trap, please.

CAROL. Me? (*Understanding—as* HE *indicates the chair.*) Oh— yes! (SHE *kneels and struggles to open the trap.*)

COLONEL. (*To* BRINDSLEY.) Well, I must say, that's very gallant of you, Miller.

BRINDSLEY. I've got a sudden touch of lumbago, sir. It often afflicts me after long spells in the dark.

CAROL. (*Very sympathetic.*) Oh, darling! Has it come back?

BRINDSLEY. I'm afraid it has, my sweet.

HAROLD. (*Opening the trap.*) Here, let me. I'm not as frail as our wilting friend. (*To* SCHUPPANZIGH.) Well, down you go, you!

SCHUPPANZIGH. (*Shrugging.*) So. Farewell. I leave the light of Art for the dark of Science.

HAROLD. Let's have a little less of your lip, shall we?

SCHUPPANZIGH. Excuse me.

(SCHUPPANZIGH *descends through the trap, taking the torch with him.* HAROLD *slams the trap door down irritably after him, and of course the lights immediately come up full. There is a long pause.* ALL *stand about embarrassed. Suddenly they hear the noise of* MISS FURNIVAL *singing "Rock of Ages" in a high drunken voice from behind the curtain. Above, attracted by the noise of the slam,* CLEA *gets out of bed, still clutching the vodka and toothmug, opens the door, and stands at the top of the stairs listening.*)

BRINDSLEY. None of this evening is happening.

CAROL. Cheer up, darling. In a few minutes everything will be all right. Mr. Bamberger will arrive in the light—he'll adore your work and give you twenty thousand pounds for your whole collection.

BRINDSLEY. (*Sarcastic.*) Oh, yes!

CAROL. Then we can buy a super Georgian house and live what's laughingly known as happily ever after. I want to leave this place just as soon as we're married.

(CLEA *hears this. Her mouth opens wide.*)

BRINDSLEY. (*Nervously.*) Sssh!

CAROL. Why? I don't want to live in a slum for our first couple of years—like other newlyweds.

BRINDSLEY. Sssh! Ssssh! . . .

CAROL. What's the matter with you?

[105]

BRINDSLEY. The gods listen, darling. They've given me a terrible night so far. They may do worse.

CAROL. (*Cooing.*) I know, darling. You've had a filthy evening. Poor babykins. But I'll fight them with you. I don't care a fig for those naughty old Goddipegs. (*Looking up.*) Do you hear? Not a single little fig!

(CLEA *aims at the voice and sends a jet of vodka splashing down over* CAROL.)

Ahh!!!

BRINDSLEY. What is it?

CAROL. It's raining!

BRINDSLEY. Don't be ridiculous.

CAROL. I'm all wet!

BRINDSLEY. How can you be?

(CLEA *throws vodka over a wider area.* HAROLD *gets it.*)

HAROLD. Hey, what's going on?

BRINDSLEY. What?

COLONEL. What the devil's the matter with you all? What are you hollerin' for? (HE *gets a slug of vodka in the face.*) Ahh!!

BRINDSLEY. (*Inspired.*) It's a leak—the water mains must have gone now.

HAROLD. Oh good God!

BRINDSLEY. It must be!

(*Mischievously,* CLEA *raps her bottle on the top stair. There is a terrified silence.* ALL *look up.*)

HAROLD. Don't say there's someone else here.

BRINDSLEY. Good Lord!

COLONEL. Who's there?

(*Silence from above.*)

Come on! I know you're there!

BRINDSLEY. (*Improvising wildly.*) I—I bet you it's Mrs. Punnet.
(CLEA *looks astonished.*)

COLONEL. Who?

BRINDSLEY. (*For* CLEA's *benefit.*) Mrs. Punnet. My cleaning
woman.

HAROLD. Cleaning woman?

BRINDSLEY. She does for me on Mondays, Wednesdays, and Fri-
days.

CAROL. Well, what would she be doing here now?

BRINDSLEY. I've just remembered—she rang up and said she'd
look in about six to tidy up the place.

COLONEL. Dammit, man, it's almost eleven.

HAROLD. She's not that conscientious. She couldn't be!

CAROL. Not these days!

COLONEL. Well, we'll soon see. (*Calling up.*) Mrs. Punnet?

BRINDSLEY. (*Desperately.*) Don't interrupt her, sir. She doesn't
like to be disturbed when she's working. Why don't we just
leave her to potter around upstairs with her duster?

COLONEL. Let us first just see if it's her. Is that you, Mrs.
Punnet? . . .

(CLEA *keeps still.*)

COLONEL. (*Roaring.*) MRS. PUNNET!

CLEA. (*Deciding on a cockney voice of great antiquity.*) 'Allo!
Yes?

BRINDSLEY. (*Weakly.*) It is. Good heavens, Mrs. Punnet, what
on earth are you doing up there?

CLEA. I'm just giving your bedroom a bit of a tidy, sir.

BRINDSLEY. At this time of night?

(*The mischief in* CLEA *begins to take over.*)

CLEA. Better late than never, sir, as they say. I know how you
like your bedroom to be nice and inviting when you're giving one of your parties.

[107]

BRINDSLEY. Yes, yes, yes, of course . . .

COLONEL. When did you come, madam?

CLEA. Just a few minutes ago, sir. I didn't like to disturb you,
so I come on up 'ere.

HAROLD. Was it you pouring all that water on us, then?

CLEA. Water? Good 'eavens, I must have upset something.
It's as black as Newgate's Knocker up 'ere. Are you playing
one of your saucy games, Mr. Miller?

BRINDSLEY. No, Mrs. Punnet. We've had a fuse. It's all over the
house.

CLEA. Oh! A *fuse!* I thought it might be one of them saucy
games in the dark, sir: Sardines or Piccadilly. The kind that
end in a general squeeze-up. I know you're rather partial
to kinky games, Mr. Miller, so I just wondered. (SHE *starts
to come down the stairs.*)

BRINDSLEY. (*Distinctly.*) It is a fuse, Mrs. Punnet. The man's
mending it now. The lights will be on *any minute!*

CLEA. Well, that'll be a relief for you, won't it? (SHE *dashes
the vodka accurately in his face, passes him by and comes
into the room.*)

BRINDSLEY. Yes, of course. Now why don't you just go on
home?

CLEA. I'm sorry I couldn't come before, sir. I was delayed, you
see. My Rosie's been taken queer again.

BRINDSLEY. I quite understand! (HE *gropes around trying to
hide her, but* SHE *continuously evades him.*)

CLEA. (*Relentlessly.*) It's her tummy. There's a lump under her
belly button the size of a grapefruit.

HAROLD. Oh how nasty!

CLEA. Horrid. Poor little Rosie. I said to her this evening, I
said, "There's no good your being mulish, my girl. You're

going to the hospital first thing tomorrow morning and getting yourself ultra-violated!"

BRINDSLEY. Well, hadn't you better be getting back to poor little Rosie! She must need you, surely?—And there's really nothing you can do here tonight.

CLEA. (*Meaningfully.*) Are you sure of that, sir?

BRINDSLEY. Positive, thank you.

(THEY *are close now.*)

CLEA. I mean, I know what this place can be like after one of your evenings. A gypsy caravan isn't in it. Gin bottles all over the floor! Bras and panties in the sink! And God knows what in the ——

(BRINDSLEY *muzzles her with his hand.* SHE *bites it hard, and* HE *drops to his knees in silent agony.*)

COLONEL. Please watch what you say, madam. You don't know it, but you're in the presence of Mr. Miller's fiancée.

CLEA. Fiancée?

COLONEL. Yes, and I am her father.

CLEA. Well, I never . . . Oh, Mr. Miller! I'm so 'appy for you! . . . Fiancée! Oh, sir! And you never told me!

BRINDSLEY. I was keeping it a surprise.

CLEA. Well, I never! Oh, how lovely! . . . May I kiss you sir, please?

BRINDSLEY. (*On his knees.*) Well yes, yes, of course . . .

(CLEA *gropes for his ear, finds it and twists it.*)

CLEA. Oh sir, I'm so pleased for you! And for *you*, Miss, too!

CAROL. Thank you.

CLEA. (*To* COLONEL MELKETT.) And for *you*, sir.

COLONEL. Thank you.

CLEA. You must be Miss Clea's father.

COLONEL. Miss Clea? I don't understand.

(*Triumphantly* SHE *sticks out her tongue at* BRINDSLEY, *who collapses his length on the floor, face down, in a gesture of total surrender. For him it is the end. The evening can hold no further disasters for him.*)

CLEA. (*To* CAROL.) Well, I never! So you've got him at last! Well done, Miss Clea! I never thought you would—not after four years . . .

BRINDSLEY. No—no—no—no. . . .

CLEA. Forgive me, sir, if I'm speaking out of turn, but you must admit four years is a long time to be courting one woman. Four days is stretching it a bit nowadays!

BRINDSLEY. (*Weakly.*) Mrs. Punnet, *please!*

CAROL. Four years!

CLEA. Well, yes, dear. It's been all of that and a bit more really, hasn't it? (*In a stage whisper.*) And of course it's just in time. It was getting a bit prominent, your little bun in the oven.

(CAROL *screeches with disgust.* BRINDSLEY *covers his ears.*)

Oh, Miss, I don't mean that's why he popped the question. Of course it's not. He's always been stuck on you. He told me so, not one week ago, in this room. (*Sentimentally.*) "Mrs. Punnet," he says, "Mrs. Punnet, as far as I'm concerned you can keep the rest of them—Miss Clea will always be on top of the heap for me." "Oh," I says, "then what about that debutante bit, Carol, the one you're always telling me about?" "Oh, 'er," he says, "she's just a bit of Knightsbridge candyfloss. A couple of licks and you've 'ad 'er."

(*There is a long pause.* CLEA *is now sitting on the table, swinging her vodka bottle in absolute command of the situation.*)

COLONEL. (*Faintly; at last grappling with the situation.*) Did you say four years, madam?

CLEA. (*In her own voice, quiet.*) Yes, Colonel. Four years, in this room.

HAROLD. I know that voice. It's Clea!

MISS FURNIVAL. (*Surprised.*) Clea!

CAROL. (*Horrified.*) Clea!

BRINDSLEY. (*Unconvincingly surprised.*) Clea!

CLEA. Surprised, Brin?

CAROL. (*Understanding.*) Clea! . . .

COLONEL. I don't understand anything that's going on in this room.

CLEA. I know. It is a very odd room, isn't it? It's like a magic dark room, where everything happens the wrong way round. Rain falls indoors, the Daily comes at night and turns in a second from a nice maid into nasty mistress.

BRINDSLEY. Be quiet, Clea!

CLEA. At last! One real word of protest! Have you finished lying, then? Have you eaten the last crumb of humble pie? Oh you coward, you bloody coward! Just because you didn't want to marry me, did you have to settle for this lot?

CAROL. Marry!

COLONEL. Marry?

CLEA. Four years of meaning to end in this triviality! Miss Laughingly Known As and her Daddipegs!

CAROL. Stop her! She's disgusting.

COLONEL. How can I, for God's sake?

CAROL. Well, where's all that bloody resource you keep talking about?

(*The* COLONEL *goes to her but takes* CLEA's *hand by mistake.*)

COLONEL. Now calm down, Dumpling. Keep your head . . . There—hold my hand, that's it, now Daddy's here. Everything is under control. All right?

CLEA. Are you sure that is your daughter's hand you're holding, Colonel?

COLONEL. What? Carol, isn't this your hand?

CAROL. No.

CLEA. You must have lived with your daughter for well over twenty years, Colonel. What remarkable use you've made of your eyes.

(*There is another pause. The* COLONEL *moves away in embarrassment.*)

CLEA. (*Wickedly.*) All right! Kinky game time! . . . Let's all play Guess the Hand.

HAROLD. Oh good God!

CLEA. Or would you rather Guess the Lips, Harold?

CAROL. How disgusting!

CLEA. Well, that's me, dear. (CAROL'*s accent.*) I'm Queen Disgustipegs!

(SHE *seizes* CAROL'*s hand and puts it into* HAROLD'*s.*) Who's that?

CAROL. I don't know.

CLEA. Guess.

CAROL. I don't know, and I don't care.

CLEA. Oh go on. Have a go!

CAROL. It's Brin, of course: You can't trick me like that! It's Brindsley's stupid hand.

HAROLD. I'm afraid you're wrong. It's me.

CAROL. (*Struggling.*) It's not. You're lying.

HAROLD. (*Holding on.*) I'm not. I don't lie.

CAROL. You're lying! . . . You're lying!

HAROLD. I'm not.

(CAROL *breaks away and blunders upstage.* SHE *is becoming hysterical.*)

CLEA. You try it, Harold. Take the hand on your right.

HAROLD. I'm not playing. It's a bloody silly game.

CLEA. Go on . . .

(SHE *seizes his hand and puts it into* BRINDSLEY'S.)

Well?

HAROLD. It's Brin.

BRINDSLEY. Yes.

CLEA. Well done! (SHE *sits on the low stool.*)

CAROL. (*Outraged.*) How does he know that? How does *he* know your hand and I don't?

BRINDSLEY. Calm down, Carol.

CAROL. Answer me! I want to know!

BRINDSLEY. Stop it!

CAROL. I won't!

BRINDSLEY. You're getting hysterical!

CAROL. Leave me alone! I want to go home.

(*And suddenly* MISS FURNIVAL *gives a sharp short scream and blunders out through the curtains.*)

MISS FURNIVAL. Prams! Prams! Prams—in the supermarket! . . .

(THEY *all freeze.* SHE *is evidently out of control in a world of her own fears.* SHE *speaks quickly and strangely.*)

All those hideous wire prams full of babies and bottles—cornflakes over there, is all they say—and then they leave you to yourself. Biscuits over there—cat food over there—fish cakes over there—Airwick over there. Pink stamps, green stamps, free balloons—television dinners—pay as you go out—oh, Daddy, it's awful! And then the Godless ones, the heathens in their leather jackets—laughing me to scorn! But, not for long. Oh, no! Who shall stand when He appeareth? He'll strike them from their motorcycles! He'll dash their helmets to the ground! Yea, verily, I say unto thee—there shall be an end of gasoline! An end to cigarette puffing and

jostling with hips . . . Keep off . . . Keep off! Keep off! . . .
(SHE *runs drunkenly across the room and collides with*
HAROLD.)

HAROLD. Come on, Ferny, I think it's time we went home.

MISS FURNIVAL. (*Pulling herself together.*) Yes. You're quite
right . . . (*With an attempt at grandeur.*) I'm sorry I can't
stay any longer, Mr. Miller; but your millionaire is unpar-
donably late. So typical of modern manners . . . Express my
regrets, if you please.

BRINDSLEY. Certainly.

(*Leaning heavily on* HAROLD's *arm* SHE *leaves the room.* HE
shuts the door after them.)

Thank you, Clea. Thank you very much.

CLEA. Any time.

BRINDSLEY. You had no right.

CLEA. No?

BRINDSLEY. *You* walked out on *me.* (HE *joins her on the low
stool.*)

CLEA. Is that what I did?

BRINDSLEY. You said you never wanted to see me again.

CLEA. I never saw you at all—how could you be walked out on?
You should live in the dark, Brindsley. It's your natural ele-
ment.

BRINDSLEY. Whatever that means.

CLEA. It means you don't really want to be seen. Why is that,
Brindsley? Do you think if someone really saw you, they
would never love you?

BRINDSLEY. Oh go away.

CLEA. I want to know.

BRINDSLEY. Yes, you always want to know. Pick-pick-pick away!
Why is *that*, Clea? Have you ever thought why you need to
do it? Well?

CLEA. Perhaps because I care about you.

BRINDSLEY. Perhaps there's nothing to care about. Just a fake artist.

CLEA. Stop pitying yourself. It's always your vice. I told you when I met you: you could either be a good artist, or a chic fake. You didn't like it, because I refused just to give you applause.

BRINDSLEY. God knows, you certainly did that!

CLEA. Is that what *she* gives you? Twenty hours of ego-massage every day?

BRINDSLEY. At least our life together isn't the replica of the Holy Inquisition you made of ours. I didn't have an affair with you: it was just four years of nooky with Torquemada!

CLEA. And don't say you didn't enjoy it!

BRINDSLEY. Enjoy it? I hated every second of it.

CLEA. Yes, I remember.

BRINDSLEY. Every second.

CLEA. I recall.

BRINDSLEY. When you left for Finland, it was the happiest day of my life.

CLEA. Mine, too!

BRINDSLEY. I sighed with relief.

CLEA. So did I.

BRINDSLEY. I went out dancing that very night.

CLEA. So did I. It was out with the lyre and the timbrel.

BRINDSLEY. Good. Then that's all right.

CLEA. Fine.

BRINDSLEY. Super!

CLEA. Duper!

BRINDSLEY. It's lovely to see you looking so happy.

CLEA. You too. Radiant with self-fulfilment.

(*A pause.*)

BRINDSLEY. If you felt like this, why did you come back?

[115]

CLEA. If *you* felt like this, why did you tell Mrs. Punnet I was still at the top of the heap?

BRINDSLEY. I never said that!

CLEA. You did.

BRINDSLEY. Never!

CLEA. You *did!*

BRINDSLEY. Of course I didn't. You invented that ten minutes ago, when you were *playing* Mrs. Punnet.

CLEA. I—Oh! So I did! . . .

(THEY *both giggle.* SHE *falls happily against his shoulder.*)

BRINDSLEY. You know something—I'm not sure she's not right. (*During this exchange the* COLONEL *and his* DAUGHTER *have been standing frozen with astonished anger. Now the outraged* FATHER *takes over.*)

COLONEL. No doubt this is very funny to you two.

CLEA. It is, quite, actually.

COLONEL. I'm not so easily amused, however, madam.

BRINDSLEY. Now look, Colonel—

COLONEL. Hold your tongue, sir, I'm talking. Do you know what would have happened to a young man in my day who dared to treat a girl the way you have treated my Dumpling?

BRINDSLEY. Well, I assume, Colonel—

COLONEL. Hold your tongue, I'm talking.

CAROL. Oh, leave it, Daddy. Let's just go home.

COLONEL. In a moment, Dumpling. Kindly leave this to me.

BRINDSLEY. Look, Carol, I can explain—

CAROL. Explain what?

BRINDSLEY. It's impossible here.

COLONEL. You understate, sir.

BRINDSLEY. Carol, you don't understand.

CAROL. What the hell's there to understand? All the time you were going with me, she was in the background—that's all

there is to it—What were you doing? Weighing us up? . . .
Here! (SHE *pulls off her engagement ring.*)

BRINDSLEY. What?

CAROL. Your ring. Take the bloody thing back!

(SHE *throws it. It hits the* COLONEL *in the eye.*)

COLONEL. My eye! My damned eye!

(CLEA *starts to laugh again.*
In mounting fury, clutching his eye.)

Oh very droll, madam! Very droll indeed! Laugh your fill!
Miller! I asked you a question. Do you know what would
have happened to a young lout like you in my day?

BRINDSLEY. Happened, sir?

COLONEL. (*Quietly.*) You'd have been thrashed, sir.

BRINDSLEY. (*Nervous.*) Thrashed—

(*The* MAN OF WAR *begins to go after him, feeling his way in*
the dark—like some furious robot.)

COLONEL. You'd have felt the mark of a father's horsewhip
across your seducer's shoulders. You'd have gone down on
your cad's bended knees, and begged my daughter's pardon
for the insults you've offered her tonight.

BRINDSLEY. (*Retreating before the* COLONEL'*s groping advance.*)
Would I, sir?

COLONEL. You'd have raised your guttersnipe voice in a piteous
scream for mercy and forgiveness!

(*A terrible scream is heard from the hall.* THEY *freeze, listen-*
ing as it comes nearer and nearer, then the door is flung open
and HAROLD *plunges into the room.* HE *is wild-eyed with rage:*
a lit and bent taper shakes in his furious hand.)

HAROLD. Ooooooh! You villain!

BRINDSLEY. Harold—

HAROLD. You skunky, conniving little villain!

BRINDSLEY. What's the matter?

HAROLD. (*Raging.*) Have you seen the state of my room? My room? My lovely room, the most elegant and cared for in this entire district?—one chair turned absolutely upside down, one chair on top of another like a Portobello junkshop! And that's not all, is it, Brindsley? Oh no, that's not the worst by a long chalk, is it, Brindsley?

BRINDSLEY. Long chalk?

HAROLD. Don't play the innocent with me. I thought I had a friend living all these years. I didn't know I was living opposite a Light-fingered Lenny!

BRINDSLEY. Harold!—

HAROLD. (*Hysterical.*) This is my reward, isn't it?—After years of looking after you, sweeping and tidying up this place, because you're too much of a slut to do it for yourself—to have my best pieces stolen from me to impress your new girl friend and her daddy. Or did she help you?

BRINDSLEY. Harold, it was an emergency.

HAROLD. Don't talk to me: I don't want to know! I know what you think of me now . . . "Don't tell Harold about the engagement. He's not to be trusted. He's not a friend. He's just someone to steal things from!"

BRINDSLEY. You know that's not true.

HAROLD. (*Shrieking—in one hysterical breath.*) I know I was the last one to know—that's what I know! I have to find it out in a room full of strangers. Me, who's listened to more of your miseries in the small hours of the morning than anyone else would put up with! All your boring talk about women, hour after hour, as if no one's got troubles but you!—

CLEA. She's getting hysterical, dear. Ignore her.

HAROLD. It's you who's going to be ignored, Clea. (*To* BRINDS-

[118]

LEY.) As for you, all I can say about your engagement is this: you deserve each other, you and that little nit.

(CAROL *gives a shriek.*)

BRINDSLEY. Carol!

HAROLD. Oh, so you're there, are you?—Skulking in the shadows!

BRINDSLEY. Leave her alone!

HAROLD. I'm not going to touch her. I just want my things and I'll be off. Did you hear me, Brindsley? You give me my things now, or I'll call the police.

BRINDSLEY. Don't be ridiculous.

HAROLD. (*Grimly.*) Item: One lyre-back Regency chair, in lacquered mahogany with Ormolu inlay and appliqué work on the cushions.

BRINDSLEY. In front of you. (HE *thrusts the taper at it.*)

HAROLD. Ta. Item: One half-back sofa—likewise Regency—supported by claw legs and upholstered in a rich silk of bottle green to match the aforesaid chair.

BRINDSLEY. In the studio.

HAROLD. Unbelievable! Item: One Coalport vase, dated 1809, decorated on the rim with a pleasing design of daisies and peonies.

BRINDSLEY. On the floor.

HAROLD. Ta.

(BRINDSLEY *hands it to him.*)

Ooooh! You've even taken the flowers! I'll come back for the chair and sofa in a minute. (*Drawing himself up with all the offended dignity of which a* HAROLD GORRINGE *is capable.*) This is the end of our relationship, Brindsley. We won't be speaking again, I don't think.

(HE *twitches his raincoat off the table. Inside it, of course, is the Buddha, which falls on the floor and smashes beyond repair. There is a terrible silence. Trying to keep his voice under control:*)

Do you know what that statue was worth? Do you? More money than you'll ever see in your whole life, even if you sell every piece of that nasty, rusty rubbish. (*With the quietness of the mad.*) I think I'm going to have to smash you, Brindsley.

BRINDSLEY. (*Nervously.*) Now steady on, Harold . . . don't be rash . . .

HAROLD. Yes, I'm very much afraid I'll have to smash you . . . Smash for smash—that's fair do's. (HE *pulls one of the long metal prongs out of the sculpture.*) Smash for smash. Smash for *smash!*

(*Insanely* HE *advances on* BRINDSLEY *holding the prong like a sword, the taper burning in his other hand.*)

BRINDSLEY. (*Retreating.*) Stop it, Harold. You've gone mad!

COLONEL. Well done, sir. I think it's time for the reckoning.

(*The* COLONEL *grabs the other prong and also advances.*)

BRINDSLEY. (*Retreating from them* BOTH.) Now just a minute, Colonel. Be reasonable! . . . Let's not revert to savages! . . . Harold, I appeal to you—you've always had civilized instincts! Don't join the Army! . . .

CAROL. (*Grimly advancing also.*) Get him, Daddy! Get him! Get him!

BRINDSLEY. (*Horrified at her.*) Carol!

CAROL. (*Malevolently.*) Get him! Get him! Get him! Get . . .

BRINDSLEY. *Clea!*

(CLEA *leaps up and blows out the taper. Lights up.*)

COLONEL. Dammit!

(CLEA *grabs* BRINDSLEY'S *hand and pulls him out of danger. To* CLEA.)

Careful, my little Dumpling. Keep out of the way.

HAROLD. (*To* CAROL.) Hush up, Colonel. We'll be able to hear them breathing.

COLONEL. Clever idea! Smart tactics, sir!

(*Silence.* THEY *listen.* BRINDSLEY *climbs carefully onto the table and silently pulls* CLEA *up after him.* HAROLD *and the* COLONEL, *prodding and slashing the darkness with their swords, grimly hunt their quarry. Twenty seconds. Suddenly, with a bang* SCHUPPANZIGH *opens the trap from below.* BOTH MEN *advance on it warily. The* ELECTRICIAN *disappears again below.* THEY *have almost reached it, on tiptoe, when there is another crash—this time from the hall.* SOMEONE *has again tripped over the milk bottles.* HAROLD *and the* COLONEL *immediately swing round and start stalking upstage, still on tiptoe.*

Enter GEORG BAMBERGER. HE *is quite evidently a millionaire. Dressed in the Gulbenkian manner,* HE *wears a beard, an eyeglass, a frock coat, a top hat and an orchid.* HE *carries a large deaf aid.*

Bewildered, HE *advances into the room. Stealthily, the* TWO *armed* MEN *stalk him upstage as* HE *silently gropes his way downstage and passes between them.*)

BAMBERGER. (*Speaking in a middle-aged German voice, as near to the voice of* SCHUPPANZIGH *as possible.*) Hallo, please! Mr. Miller?

(HAROLD *and the* COLONEL *spin round in a third direction.*)

HAROLD. Oh, it's the electrician!

BAMBERGER. Hallo, please?

COLONEL. What the devil are you doing up here?

(SCHUPPANZIGH *appears at the trap.*)

Have you mended the fuse?

HAROLD. Or are you going to keep us in the dark all night?

SCHUPPANZIGH. Don't worry. The fuse is mended.

(HE *comes out of the trap.*

BAMBERGER *goes round the stage, right.*)

HAROLD. Thank God for that.

BAMBERGER. (*Still groping around.*) Hallo, please? Mr. Miller—vere are you? Vy zis darkness? Is a joke, yes?

SCHUPPANZIGH. (*Incensed.*) Ah, no! That is not very funny, good people—just because I am a foreigner, to imitate my voice. You English can be the rudest people on earth!

BAMBERGER. (*Imperiously.*) Mr. Miller! I have come here to give attention to your sculptures!

SCHUPPANZIGH. *Gott in himmel!*

BAMBERGER. *Gott in himmel!*

BRINDSLEY. God, it's him! Bamberger!

CLEA. He's come!

HAROLD. Bamberger!

COLONEL. Bamberger!

(THEY *freeze. The* MILLIONAIRE *sets off, left, toward the open trap.*)

BRINDSLEY. Don't worry, Mr. Bamberger. We've had a fuse, but it's mended now.

BAMBERGER. (*Irritably.*) Mr. Miller!

CLEA. You'll have to speak up. He's deaf.

BRINDSLEY. (*Shouting.*) Don't worry, Mr. Bamberger! We've had a fuse, but it's all right now! . . .

(*Standing on the table,* HE *clasps* CLEA *happily.* BAMBERGER *misses the trap by inches.*)

Oh, Clea, that's true. Everything's all right now! Just in the nick of time!

(*But as* HE *says this* BAMBERGER *turns and falls into the open trap door.* SCHUPPANZIGH *slams it to with his foot.*)

SCHUPPANZIGH. So! Here's now an end to your troubles! Like

Jehovah in the Sacred Testament, I give you the most mirac-
ulous gift of the Creation! Light!

CLEA. Light!

BRINDSLEY. Oh, thank God. *Thank God!*

(SCHUPPANZIGH *goes to the switch.*)

HAROLD. (*Grimly.*) I wouldn't thank Him too soon, Brindsley,
if I were you!

COLONEL. Nor would I, Brindsley, if I were you!

CAROL. Nor would I, Brinnie Winnie, if I were you!

SCHUPPANZIGH. (*Grandly.*) Then thank *me!* For I shall play God
for this second! (*Clapping his hands.*) Attend all of you.
God said: "Let there be light!" And there was, good people,
suddenly!—astoundingly!—instantaneously!—inconceivably—
inexhaustibly—inextinguishably and eternally—LIGHT!

(SCHUPPANZIGH, *with a great flourish, flicks the light switch.
INSTANT DARKNESS. The turntable of the phonograph
starts up again, and with an exultant crash the Sousa march
falls on the audience—and blazes away in the black.*)

END

SCAVENGER HUNT HEIST

Don't miss any of the cases in the Hardy Boys Clue Book series!

#1: *The Video Game Bandit*

#2: *The Missing Playbook*

#3: *Water-Ski Wipeout*

#4: *Talent Show Tricks*

Coming Soon

#6: *A Skateboard Cat-astrophe*

HARDY BOYS

→ Clue Book ←

#5

SCAVENGER HUNT HEIST

BY FRANKLIN W. DIXON ⇆ ILLUSTRATED BY MATT DAVID

ALADDIN
NEW YORK   LONDON   TORONTO   SYDNEY   NEW DELHI

An imprint of Simon & Schuster Children's Publishing Division
1230 Avenue of the Americas, New York, NY 10020
First Aladdin hardcover edition April 2017
Text copyright © 2017 by Simon & Schuster, Inc.
Illustrations copyright © 2017 by Matt David
Also available in an Aladdin paperback edition.
All rights reserved, including the right of reproduction in whole or in part in any form.
ALADDIN and related logo are registered trademarks of Simon & Schuster, Inc.
THE HARDY BOYS and colophons are registered trademarks of Simon & Schuster, Inc.
HARDY BOYS CLUE BOOK and colophons are trademarks of Simon & Schuster, Inc.
For information about special discounts for bulk purchases, please contact
Simon & Schuster Special Sales at 1-866-506-1949 or business@simonandschuster.com.
The Simon & Schuster Speakers Bureau can bring authors to your live event.
For more information or to book an event contact the Simon & Schuster Speakers Bureau
at 1-866-248-3049 or visit our website at www.simonspeakers.com.
Book designed by Karina Granda
The text of this book was set in Adobe Garamond Pro.
Manufactured in the United States of America 0317 FFG
2 4 6 8 10 9 7 5 3 1
Library of Congress Control Number 2016954902
ISBN 978-1-4814-8517-3 (hc)
ISBN 978-1-4814-8516-6 (pbk)
ISBN 978-1-4814-8518-0 (eBook)

CONTENTS

CHAPTER 1   FOFT   1

CHAPTER 2   BEE CAREFUL!   9

CHAPTER 3   BEARY SCARY   16

CHAPTER 4   A CRIME AGAINST CANDY   28

CHAPTER 5   SWORD FIGHT!   36

CHAPTER 6   OOEY CLUEY   45

CHAPTER 7   TREE HUGGER   53

CHAPTER 8   STAY BACK!   60

CHAPTER 9   DON'T FEED THE ANIMALS   67

CHAPTER 10 THE BEAR TRUTH   79

Chapter 1

FOFT

"Rawwwr!"

Frank Hardy jumped nearly a foot in the air, splashing the milk from his cereal bowl all over his brand-new navy-blue T-shirt. "Joe! That's not funny!"

"It's not?" Eight-year-old Joe Hardy disagreed. In fact, he was laughing so hard, he thought orange juice would come out his nose. "Don't worry, Frank. I know I do a killer bear impression, but it's just me."

He laughed some more while his brother grumbled under his breath.

"Joe Hardy!"

Joe's laughter died in his throat as soon as he heard his father, Fenton Hardy, shout his name.

"Stop teasing your brother," Mr. Hardy said, peering at Joe over his newspaper. But Joe thought he saw a smile in his father's eyes.

Frank refilled his bowl of Healthy Nut Crunch with fresh milk and took a seat back at the breakfast table with Joe and Mr. Hardy.

"I'm not teasing Frank," explained Joe, slurping the sweet milk from his bowl of Sugar-O's. "I'm helping him face his fears."

"I'm not afraid!" said Frank. But when he looked at his watch and saw that he would be at Bayport Bear Park, along with the other third and fourth graders, in less than an hour, he shivered.

In his nine years, Frank had faced a lot of fears solving mysteries with his younger brother, Joe, and their friends—their dad had even built them a tree house, which served as their official mystery-solving headquarters. But so far, Frank had never faced an actual bear—and he'd hoped he never would. He'd seen a show about bears on TV last year. They were huge, and could smell people, animals, and food from miles away! Not to mention that when they defended themselves, they stood on their back legs and their fur puffed out so they could look extra big!

Suddenly Frank felt a little queasy. "Dad," he moaned, cradling his stomach with one hand. "I don't feel so good."

"No?" Mr. Hardy said. "What's wrong, Frank?"

"He's got FOFT," said Joe, rolling his eyes.

"FOFT?" asked Mr. Hardy.

"Fear of Field Trip," Joe said, cracking a smile in his brother's direction.

"Not that Frank *is* afraid," said Mrs. Hardy, entering the kitchen. "But you two know that you won't have to see any real bears at Bear Park, right? It's just a silly name." She kissed Frank on the top of his head and handed him a fresh T-shirt, which he swapped for his soggy one right at the table.

"Or is it?" Joe waggled his eyebrows up and down dramatically.

Even Frank had to laugh at his brother's ridiculous face this time.

"Dad," Frank said, deciding that it was time for a change of subject. "Do you have any cases for work that you need our help with?"

Fenton Hardy was a private detective, and sometimes he worked with the local Bayport Police Department to help solve crimes. When he needed their help, Mr. Hardy was known to tell Frank and Joe about the cases he worked on; he knew the boys had their own detective club and had solved lots of mysteries of their own.

Mr. Hardy showed his sons the front page of the newspaper he was reading. The headline on the front, in big black letters, read: NY POLICE HUNT FOR JEWEL HEIST ROBBERS!

"A jewel heist!" Joe exclaimed, through a mouthful of Sugar-O's. "Cool!"

"Do you have any leads?" Frank asked seriously.

"A couple," said Mr. Hardy. "While you're on your field trip, I'm going to be at the police station, helping the officers question a suspect."

"Why don't you just arrest him?" asked Joe.

"Because first we have to make sure he committed the crime," said Mr. Hardy. "Remember last year when Joe thought Mrs. Beasley next door stole his bike?"

Frank laughed, his eyes sparkling. "And we found it the next day, in the backyard. Joe forgot he left it there."

"Honest mistake," Joe defended himself. "She was acting suspicious."

"Exactly," said Mr. Hardy. "But if you'd accused

Mrs. Beasley without proof, you'd have looked awfully silly. Same with the jewel heist. Before we arrest someone, we need to have proof he did it, otherwise the real bad guy could get away with robbing that jewelry store."

Frank thought about this for a minute, then took out a pocket notebook that Aunt Trudy had gotten him. Frank and Joe liked to take notes when they were solving a mystery, and this seemed like a very good first note to make in his notebook. *Proof!* he wrote.

"You boys better get a move on," Mrs. Hardy said, pointing at their kitchen clock. "The school bus will be here in ten minutes, and you don't want to miss your field trip."

Frank closed his notebook and placed it in his back pocket. He couldn't help but wonder if missing the field trip was really such a bad thing.

"Watch it, Hardys!" Adam Ackerman, the biggest bully at Bayport Elementary School, pushed past Frank and Joe on his way out of the school bus, stepping on Joe's toes as he went.

They had just arrived at Bayport Bear Park, and Adam was cutting past everyone to make sure he was the first one off the bus.

"Even I waited my turn," Cissy Zermeño told Frank and Joe as they climbed down off the school bus. "And I like to be first and best at everything."

Frank and Joe exchanged a look. No one knew how Cissy liked to be number one better than the Hardys. She always won at everything.

"Okay, everyone," Ms. Potter, one of the chaperones (and a teacher at Bayport Elementary), called out. "Please follow me into the visitors' cabin, single file."

Frank had to admit the park was pretty neat. It was springtime, so everything was green and bright and the birds were singing their chipper songs. After a long winter, it was nice to see leaves on the trees again, and clover-green grass covered the ground. A few picnic tables and grills for cookouts dotted the park. On the outskirts of the property was a thick, sprawling forest with all different kinds of trees.

That must be where the bears live, thought Frank, his heart pounding.

Straight ahead, Ms. Potter led the line of students into a dark-brown log-cabin-type building. In front of it was a wooden sign that said BAYPORT BEAR PARK VISITORS' CABIN.

Inside the cabin, Joe's classmates were crowded around something that he couldn't see.

"Whoa," said Phil Cohen, one of the Hardys' best friends. "Look at that!"

"What is it?" asked Joe, inching toward the center of the crowd.

That was when Frank and Joe saw it—a big yellow ball about the size and shape of a watermelon, covered in bumblebees!

Chapter 2

BEE CAREFUL!

"Get back!" Frank said, holding his hand out in front of his brother for protection. "It's a beehive!"

"You scaredy-cat!" Adam Ackerman taunted, laughing loudly. "It's not a real beehive!"

"Then what is it?" Joe asked, crossing his arms over his chest. Now that he was closer, he could see that the beehive and the bees attached to it were fake—they looked like they were made out of colored paper of some sort. Still, he didn't know what it was or why it was sitting on a table in the middle of the Bayport Bear Park visitors' cabin— and he was pretty sure that Adam didn't, either.

Adam's cheeks reddened. "Why should I tell you what it is?"

Phil Cohen pulled his phone out of his pocket and took a picture, then punched a few buttons. Phil was a tech whiz—he always had the latest electronic gadgets.

"According to my image recognition search," said Phil, "it's a piñata." He pronounced it *pin-ah-ta*.

"*Pin-yah-ta*," corrected Cissy. "My parents get me one every year for my birthday!"

"What's it do?" asked Joe.

"It's filled with toys and candy and stuff! You're supposed to take turns trying to break it open with a baseball bat, and when it all falls out, you get to keep the prizes."

"Did someone say *candy*?" A girl with honey-colored hair and a bubble-gum-pink hoodie spoke up, making a beeline for the piñata.

"I got here first!" Adam shouted, reaching his hand out to grab the piñata.

Fweeeeeeeeeeet!

The whole class turned toward the sound of someone blowing a whistle.

"Step away from the piñata!" There, standing next to Ms. Potter, was a teenage girl with glossy chestnut hair and a whistle around her neck. She had on a chocolate-brown uniform stitched with green letters that read HEATHER.

"She's a ranger?" Frank asked. "She sure doesn't look like one to me."

Joe shook his head. Heather wore a ranger uniform, but she was also wearing a glittery purple headband, pale-pink nail polish, and hot-pink lip gloss, and she held a cell phone in one hand.

"I'm a junior ranger here at Bear Park," Heather said. "I'll be leading your field trip today."

"But you're a girl," said Adam Ackerman, screwing up his face into a frown.

"I'm a girl who probably knows more about this park and the surrounding woods than a hundred boys put together." Heather stared Adam down. "And *you* should keep your hands off that piñata."

"What's the piñata for?" the girl with the honey-blond hair asked, wide-eyed. "Is it really filled with candy?"

"Who is that?" Joe asked his brother.

"Lolly Sugarman," said Frank. "She's in my class. She's obsessed with candy—I've never seen her without either a lollipop, a chocolate bar, or bubble gum."

"Yes, it's filled with toys and candy. And that's a good question," Heather told Lolly. "Today we're going to divide you all into teams of four. Then you're going to compete . . . in a scavenger hunt!"

There was a murmur among the students, and they immediately began grouping themselves into teams. Frank and Joe called out to their friend Chet Morton, but Heather blew her super-loud whistle and everyone went silent.

"I'll be choosing the teams," Heather said.

"Heather?" said Cissy, her arm raised high in the air. "What's a scavenger hunt?"

"It's a competition," said Heather. "I'm going to be handing out a list of five clues, and each team will have to solve the clues together."

Frank and Joe exchanged excited looks. They were the best at solving clues!

"Then," Heather continued, "you'll have to find and collect the answer to each clue in the park somewhere. For example, a clue might be: What is green with four parts and brings you luck—"

"A four-leaf clover!" shouted Cissy.

"Right." Heather nodded. "So you would have to find a four-leaf clover somewhere in the park. We'll be handing out plastic bags with the clues so you can store your scavenger hunt items as you go."

"How do we know who wins?" asked Cissy.

Heather twirled a lock of hair around her finger. "The winning team is the one that collects all the scavenger hunt items first. Winners get to break open the piñata and divide up the candy and prizes among themselves."

The students began chattering eagerly. Frank was excited about the toy prizes inside, whereas

Joe was more excited about the candy. If they won, they'd know just how to divide up their piñata winnings!

Heather divided everyone up into teams of four. Frank and Joe wound up on the same team, along with Phil Cohen and Lolly Sugarman.

"Okay," Frank said, addressing his teammates. "It looks like our biggest competition will be Cissy Zermeño. Who else is on her team?"

"Oh no," said Joe, glancing at Cissy. "Adam Ackerman is on her team."

"Poor Cissy," said Phil. "Tony Riccio and Seth Darnell are on her team too."

Tony and Seth were both friends of Adam's. They weren't as mean as Adam could be, but they weren't nice like Cissy, either. Joe felt bad for her.

Heather handed each group a set of clues in a sealed envelope, a map of the park, and a bunch of plastic bags and told them not to peek at the clues until she said so. Frank was in charge of holding the envelope for his group.

"We *have* to win," Lolly told her teammates.

"Candy is my number one favorite thing in the whole world!"

Phil looked at her. "You like candy even better than computers?"

"More than *anything*," Cissy said.

"Don't worry," Joe said, grinning. "The Hardy boys are on the case!"

"Okay!" Heather shouted. "It's time to open your—"

Just then the cabin door burst open. And there, standing in the doorway, was the biggest, tallest, scariest bear Frank Hardy had ever seen!

Chapter 3

BEARY SCARY

"Graaaawwwwwr!" a rough voice rumbled.

The class screamed.

"It's a fake!" Joe Hardy shouted, stepping forward and pointing at the figure in the doorway.

The class gasped. Frank thought he could feel his heart skip a beat.

The man in the bear suit seemed to be talking now. But all anyone could hear was *mumble, mumble, mumble.* He was still wearing his bear mask.

Heather stared at the man in the bear suit. "Your mask," she prodded, rolling her eyes.

The man laughed and removed the bear mask from his head. "Sorry about that, kids! The young man in the red shirt," he said, indicating Joe, "is right! I'm not a real bear."

"Who are you, then?" Elisa Locke asked, narrowing her eyes.

"My name is Bo Bobbleton," he said, stepping out of the bear costume. Underneath it, he wore a chocolate-brown ranger uniform, just like Heather's. He was tall and muscular, with black hair that was streaked with silver and a stubbly silver beard. Even without the costume, he looked a little bearlike. "But you can call me Ranger Bo!"

"I told you that suit would scare them!" Heather said, slipping her phone into the back pocket of her uniform.

"I wasn't scared!" Joe said. "My mom told me that we wouldn't see any *real* bears at Bear Park."

Bo nodded. "And we'd like to keep it that way, so before you begin your scavenger hunt, I'm going to go over some of our Bear Park rules and regulations. It's for your own safety."

Joe wrinkled his nose. He hated rules!

Frank didn't mind, though. Rules helped everyone stay safe.

"First," said Bo, holding up a finger like he was pointing to the sky, "you must solve the clues with your whole team, or else it doesn't count."

Joe shrugged. That one wasn't so bad.

"Second, no food or drink outside this cabin."

"Why not?" Cissy asked.

Bo and Heather exchanged a look, which made Frank curious. They sure seemed uneasy about something!

"We don't want food being left out and attracting any animals," Ranger Bo explained.

"Like . . . *bears*?" Frank gulped.

"There's no reason to be afraid of the wildlife, but keeping food and drink in the cabin and making sure you observe rule number three will ensure that there are no problems."

Problems? Frank thought. He couldn't help but notice that Ranger Bo hadn't exactly answered no. "And please don't feed the wildlife, even if they look cute," Heather added.

"What's rule number three?" Joe asked.

"No wandering off the path into the woods," said Ranger Bo.

Once the students agreed to obey the park rules, Ranger Bo counted down from three, and everyone ran outside at once, excited to look at the first clue.

Once their team was outside, Frank opened the envelope and selected a note card with *Clue #1* at the top. He showed Lolly, Joe, and Phil what it said:

Light as a _____
in all kinds of weather.
Birds use me to fly
all through the sky.

"That one's easy!" said Frank, smiling. "The answer is 'feather.'"

"Great job!" said Joe.

"But where do we find one of those?" asked Phil.

"Well," said Lolly, after blowing a huge bubble with her neon-purple bubble gum. "Birds make nests in trees. Maybe we'll find a feather near the woods?"

The team headed for the forest beyond the clearing where the visitors' cabin and picnic tables were.

"Look at this one!" said Joe, running over to a huge oak tree. It had a hole in the center of its trunk shaped like a long oval—almost like a mouth open in a yawn. Next to it was a pretty maple tree with polished-looking reddish-purple leaves.

The group searched beneath the trees. Before long, Joe found a shiny black feather lying on top of the grass under the big oak.

"Congratulations!" boomed a voice just behind them. "You found the first scavenger hunt item!"

Frank and Joe turned to find Ranger Bo beaming at their team.

"You're the first team to find the first item," added Bo.

"One step closer to all that candy," said Lolly, her eyes twinkling.

"That's right, young lady," said Ranger Bo. He walked off toward another team that was farther along the path.

Joe grinned. "We have two amateur detectives on our team," he said. "We're sure to win this thing!"

"Read the next clue, quick!" said Lolly. "I think I just saw Adam Ackerman with a white feather!"

Frank opened a plastic bag, and Joe dropped the feather in. Then Phil produced Clue #2 from the envelope and read it aloud to his team:

> *"You'll find me where pigs roll around,*
> *and where rain meets dirt.*
> *You'll find me on the ground—*
> *just don't get me on your shirt!"*

"Where pigs roll around?" asked Frank.

"Pigs are dirty," said Lolly. "But the answer can't be dirt, because the clue says that it's dirt mixed with rain."

The group thought for a minute.

"Wait," said Phil. "I think I know the answer!"

"You can't look it up on your phone," said Frank. "That's cheating."

"I didn't look it up," Phil said. "But I know that dirt and water make mud—that must be it!"

"Mud?" asked Lolly, sticking out her tongue. "Gross!"

Joe nodded, stifling his laugh—girls were so weird sometimes. "Pigs like to roll around in mud, and I know my aunt Gertrude hates when I get mud on my shirt."

"But where will we find mud around here?" asked Phil, tapping his phone. He looked at the screen and then back to his teammates. "According to the weather forecast, it hasn't rained in over three weeks."

Frank nodded. "And the only way to make mud is with water and dirt."

Joe kicked at the ground, uncovering layer after layer of dry-as-dust dirt. "Nothing," he said. "Does anyone else have any ideas?"

"It wouldn't matter where in the park we went," said Frank, unfolding a map of Bear Park that each team had been given. "If it hasn't rained and there are no lakes or streams—which, according to the map, there aren't—all the dirt would be the same."

Suddenly Lolly gasped. "I've got it!" she exclaimed, taking her backpack off her back and unzipping it.

Joe gave Frank and Phil a quizzical look.

Lolly produced a thermos from her backpack.

"There's mud in your thermos?" asked Phil.

"No, silly!" Lolly's curls dazzled in the sunlight. "My mom and I made SugarSugar Punch last weekend. All we had to do was mix the flavored powder with water."

"What does that have to do with mud?" asked Frank with a serious look on his face.

Lolly unscrewed the top of the thermos and poured the punch on the ground next to the nearby picnic table, on top of a patch of dirt. She used a stick to mix the dirt and the SugarSugar Punch together. The result was a thick brown sludge.

"She made mud!" said Phil.

"Of course!" said Frank. "The SugarSugar Punch is made from water, and water and dirt make mud!"

"Hey, Frank," said Joe. "Think fast!" Quick as lightning, Joe scooped up a handful of mud and flicked it at his brother. It landed on Frank's forehead with a splat.

At first Frank froze. But soon enough he was laughing so hard tears were rolling down his face. He retaliated by throwing a handful of mud at Phil and one at Joe.

Laughing hysterically and not wanting the only girl member of their group to feel left out, Phil smeared some mud on Lolly Sugarman's cheek. She was laughing with the rest of her team, until . . .

"My hoodie!" Lolly hollered.

A quarter-size splotch of sugar-mud had fallen from Lolly's cheek onto her soft pink hoodie.

"I'm sorry, Lolly," said Phil. "It was an accident!"

"My mom's going to be so mad," she said, chin quivering. "This is a brand-new hoodie!"

"Hey, just like the clue said!" laughed Joe.

Lolly glared at him.

"Or not," he said weakly.

Frank tried to reason with her. "Lolly, what if you tried washing it off in the restroom? Our aunt Gertrude takes stains out by running our clothes under the water faucet sometimes."

After a couple more chin quivers from Lolly,

the boys convinced her to go back to the cabin's restroom and try to the get mud out of her hoodie. But after nearly ten minutes, they were starting to get worried. What was taking so long? They wanted to open the next clue, but according to Ranger Bo's scavenger hunt rules, they all had to read and solve the clue together, or it didn't count.

"She's taking forever!" complained Joe. "What, did she fall in?"

Finally Frank, Joe, and Phil decided to follow Lolly into the cabin. After all, the other teams had probably caught up to them, so they couldn't afford to waste more time. "She must be in here somewhere," said Frank, pushing open the door to the visitors' cabin.

But all three of them stopped short, their mouths open wide in shock.

Because there, on the table where the piñata had once sat, were now only a few shreds of yellow paper—the prize piñata was missing!

Chapter 4

A CRIME AGAINST CANDY

"What happened to the candy?" Joe Hardy exclaimed. He and the others ran over to the table.

"Someone stole the piñata!" said Phil. He combed his fingers through the scraps of yellow tissue paper and little pieces that used to be the fake bumble bees attached to the hive. "I wonder what happened?"

Just then Adam Ackerman came from another part of the cabin into the main room. He wore his usual smirk, as well as a ring of dark chocolate smudged all around his lips.

"What did you losers do to my prize?" he asked. Then, upon getting a closer look at the mess on the table, he shouted, "It's gone!"

"As if you didn't know!" said Phil pointedly. "You had your hands on that piñata the second you saw it!"

Adam laughed. "Are you crazy?" he asked. "Does it *look* like I have your stupid beehive?"

"No," admitted Frank. "But it *does* look like you've eaten quite a bit of candy—which is what was *inside* the piñata."

Adam looked genuinely stumped. "I'm sick of your stupid detective club always blaming me for everything," he said.

"If you didn't eat the piñata candy," said Joe, pointing back at the table, "then what's with the chocolate mustache?"

Adam's eyes widened. He wiped his mouth on the back of his hand. "Fine," he said at last. "Ranger Bo caught me eating a chocolate bar while we were out in the woods. He made me come back to the cabin to get rid of it before it attracted any animals."

"It doesn't look like you got rid of it," Frank said, eyeing the chocolate still on Adam's face.

"He said I had to get rid of it," Adam grumbled. "He didn't say that I couldn't get rid of it in my mouth."

The restroom door slammed, and Lolly Sugarman walked out. Her pink sweatshirt still had a brown spot on it, but it was a little faded now. And wet.

"What happened?" She ran to the table and saw the few shreds of confetti, all that remained of the piñata. "My beautiful piñata full of delicious candy!" she moaned.

"Oh boy," said Joe, under his breath. "This isn't going to be pretty."

Phil explained to Lolly what had happened in the past few minutes.

"Did you see anything when you first came in, Lolly?" asked Frank. He pulled the notebook out of his pocket, along with a pen.

Lolly shook her head. "No," she said. "The piñata was still here when I walked in. I remember admiring it." She tightened her grip on her backpack.

Frank and Joe exchanged glances. Lolly was acting sort of strange—like she was uncomfortable about something.

"Was Adam here when you came in?" Joe asked.

"No, no one else was here. I noticed the back door to the cabin was open, so I thought someone might be inside—but when I called out, there was no one there. After that, I closed the door and went into the restroom to try to get the mud out." She frowned at her sweatshirt.

"See?" said Adam, scowling. "I got here five minutes before you three did. You dummies are barking up the wrong tree! Again!"

"I still say Ackerman did it," said Phil. "He's acting suspicious."

Frank looked at the first page of his new detective's notebook. It had only one word written on it, the one he'd written earlier that morning after his dad had told him about that jewel heist.

Proof!

They couldn't accuse Adam of stealing the piñata without better proof.

"Let's think this through," said Frank. "Lolly got here first, which we know because the cabin was empty when she came in. And by the time we came in, Adam was here."

"Duh," said Adam, crossing his arms over his chest.

"The piñata was still here when Lolly went into the restroom," Joe said, picking up where his brother left off. "But when we came into cabin, it was gone. Plus, Adam was here."

"If I stole the piñata," said Adam, "then where is it? And where is the candy?" He pulled his pants pockets inside out, showing everyone they were empty.

"You could have eaten it all," said Phil. "And then thrown away the piñata part."

"No, Adam's right," Lolly sighed. "In my professional candy-eating opinion, five minutes is not enough time for anyone to have eaten a whole piñata full of candy. Not even *me*."

Phil looked disappointed, but he didn't say anything.

"I guess we better tell Ranger Bo," said Frank.

After they told Ranger Bo and Heather what had happened, the two rangers convened the rest of the teams inside the cabin and made an announcement— or tried to. The students were so upset over the missing scavenger hunt prize that groans and whispers were spreading around the room quickly. Finally Ms. Potter had Heather blow her whistle, and everyone quieted down.

"Everything will go on as scheduled," said Ranger Bo.

"But what will the winner get now that there's no piñata?" asked Cissy.

"The adults will find a new prize while you kids go back to your scavenger hunt," said Bo. He patted his pockets, as though looking for something he couldn't find.

"You gave them to me for safekeeping, remember?" Heather dangled a set of keys in front of Bo's eyes.

He put a palm to his forehead. "I forgot!"

"Why don't you let me go to the store?" said Heather eagerly.

Ranger Bo looked at her like he wanted to say something, but stopped himself. Then he said, "I'll figure something out. You go ahead and help with the scavenger hunt."

"Suit yourself." She shrugged. But Bo was still

looking at her suspiciously when everyone else began looking for clues again.

"Are you thinking what I'm thinking?" Joe asked Frank.

Frank nodded. "It looks like Team Hardy has a new case to solve!"

Chapter 5

SWORD FIGHT!

After the rest of the kids had gone back outside to resume their scavenger hunt, Frank and Joe huddled up. While they huddled up, Heather was off in the corner, typing furiously on her phone.

"Let's try to get the facts down," said Frank, opening his notebook.

Joe nodded. "We've got our *what*. Now we just have to figure out the *who, when, where,* and *why*."

Frank scribbled the first *W* into their notebook, followed by the rest of the *W*s:

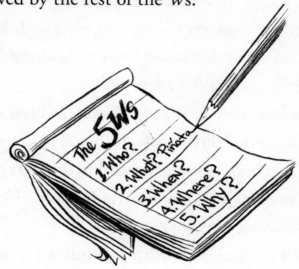

"What are you guys doing?" Lolly asked, leaning over the notebook.

"Solving a mystery," Joe said. "These are the five *W*s." He pointed to the page in front of them. "It's how we solve our cases."

"You mean you've solved mysteries before?" she asked.

"Tons of them!" Phil told her.

"Would you like to help us solve this one?" Frank asked Lolly. "We can use all the help we can get!"

"That sounds like fun . . . ," she said, trailing off. She looked out the window at the other teams, which were hard at work on the scavenger hunt. It looked like Adam, Cissy, Seth, and Tony were already starting their search for Clue #3.

"Are you worried that we'll miss the rest of the scavenger hunt?" Frank asked Lolly. He knew how much she'd been looking forward to the prize candy.

She nodded, looking down at her feet. "Not that it matters who wins anymore."

Frank nudged his brother and put the detective's notebook back in his pocket.

"C'mon," Joe said. "We can do the scavenger hunt and try to solve the mystery at the same time."

"Really?" asked Lolly, her blue eyes brightening.

"Really!" said Frank. "Besides, Ranger Bo said he was getting us a new prize."

"Even if it's not candy." Lolly sighed.

"Who cares?" Phil said. "As long as we beat Adam Ackerman!"

Frank, Joe, Lolly, and Phil went back outside and opened their third clue.

Nearby, Elisa Locke was jumping out of the way while Chet Morton poured his water bottle onto the dirt near her pretty black boots. If they hurried, they could still catch up!

Phil and the others all read the clue:

_____s and stones
will break our bones.
To hit the bull's-eye,
I'm shaped like a Y.

Lolly placed a finger on her chin. "My sister used to say that when I'd call her names."

"What?" Joe asked.

"Sticks and stones will break my bones, but words will never hurt me."

"So we're looking for a stick?" said Phil.

"Not just any stick," whispered Frank. He leaned into his teammates so none of the other teams would hear. "We need to find a Y-shaped stick!"

"Everyone else is in the woods," observed Joe. "Maybe we should look for our stick over there, near the park benches. There are trees over there, too—I'll bet a bunch of sticks have fallen on the ground underneath them."

He pointed toward a circular space in the middle of the park, where a few park benches formed a semicircle. He was right; there were trees all around the benches, shading them from the bright spring sunshine.

When they got there, everyone got down on their hands and knees and started looking for a stick in the shape of a Y.

As they searched, they talked some more about what Joe had named the Case of the Scavenger Hunt Heist, and Frank jotted down notes in his notebook.

"What about the *where*?" Joe asked. "We know that one."

"True," Frank said, winding his way around the dirt path to the woods. "The candy and piñata were taken from the visitors' cabin."

"We can keep looking while you write that down," Lolly offered helpfully.

"Thanks!" Frank said, scribbling in his notebook. While he was writing, he held the paper in place so the balmy spring wind wouldn't turn the page.

Where: Bear Park visitors' cabin

"Now all we need are the *when*, the *why*, and the *who*," he told the others.

"We know the *when*, don't we?" asked Joe. He was on his knees, sifting through a pile of twigs on the ground. Some of them were sort of wavy, but none of them looked exactly like a Y.

"It was after I went inside to get the stain off my shirt," said Lolly.

"And that was at eleven thirty," said Phil. "I remember, because I checked my watch."

Frank wrote *11:30* in his notebook.

"And ten minutes later, we followed her inside," said Phil. He knelt down on the ground and brushed aside some leaves to see if there were any Y-shaped twigs hiding underneath them—no such luck.

"So the piñata had to have been stolen between

eleven thirty and eleven forty," said Frank, making another note.

"That's not very much time," said Joe, dusting some dirt off the knees of his jeans.

"That was a big piñata," Lolly pointed out. "I wonder where it went that fast—and where the candy inside went."

"That's a good point." Frank thought for a minute and looked back at that word he'd written in the notebook earlier that morning—*Proof!* If they found the candy, he bet that they'd find proof of who'd taken the piñata.

"It has to be close by," said Joe. "The thief couldn't have gotten far with it in just ten minutes."

"Got it!" Phil shouted, pointing at a stick under a park bench.

But just as he picked it up, Seth Darnell and Tony Riccio knocked it out of his hands—with their own Y-shaped sticks!

"*En garde!*" shouted Tony, holding his stick like a sword.

Seth brandished his own stick like a sword too.

"'My name is Inigo Montoya,'" he said, quoting the movie *The Princess Bride*, which had one of Frank and Joe's very favorite sword fights of any movie, ever. "Prepare to—*ahhhhh!*"

Joe came at Seth with a stick he'd broken off a nearby tree, and the two boys toppled to the ground, laughing.

Soon all the boys were having a mock sword fight.

"You guys!" moaned Cissy, standing beside Lolly with her hands folded over her chest. "Stop! We're wasting time!"

"Yeah," added Lolly. "Stop horsing around."

"She's right," said Cissy. "We'll never win if you keep playing sword fight."

Adam charged Frank with his stick, but Frank ducked just in time. Adam ran right into the tree!

He got to his feet quickly, though, just in time to block Frank's swipe.

"Stop!" Cissy repeated. She turned to Lolly. "Boys are so dumb sometimes."

They watched as the boys continued to parry with the Y-shaped sticks.

"What should we do?" Cissy asked.

Lolly took a deep breath, then threw herself into the middle of the boys' imaginary sword fight, holding out her palms as if to say *Stop!*

Phil, who had been running at Joe with his stick-sword, ran right into Lolly, knocking her—and her backpack—to the ground.

The second it hit the ground, Lolly's backpack flew open—and heaps and heaps of candy spilled out like lava out of a volcano.

"Is that . . . ?" Phil blinked at the candy on the ground.

"A piñata's worth of candy!" Frank said.

Chapter 6

OOEY CLUEY

Lolly pushed herself up off the ground. "Now my new sweatshirt has a mud spot *and* a grass stain."

"Lolly," said Joe, eyes widening. "Where did all that candy come from?"

"Isn't it obvious?" Adam snatched the backpack out of Lolly's grasp. "Lolly Sugarman stole the scavenger hunt prize!"

Cissy gasped and ran to Adam's side, her eyes on the backpack.

"Did not!" said Lolly. She grabbed her backpack and began shoveling the spilled candy back inside. Then she paused and looked at her team.

Frank, Joe, and Phil were all gaping at the candy pieces still on the ground. None of them knew what to say—it didn't look good for Lolly.

"You believe me, don't you?" Lolly asked.

"Well . . . ," said Phil, red-faced.

"I mean, why do you have all that candy?" asked Joe.

Lolly rolled her eyes. "Guys, this is my personal candy stash. I always have it on me, at all times."

Cissy looked at her feet. "I don't know. . . ."

Lolly stood. She held a handful of the candy that had spilled out of her backpack. The wrappers were bright purple, with white polka dots. "Do you see what this is?" she asked the boys.

"Proof that Team Hardy won't be winning the scavenger hunt?" Adam asked, cackling at his own joke.

"It's Grapelicious Ooey Gooey gum," said Lolly, as if the answer was obvious.

"So?" Adam asked.

"So, I'm *always* chewing Grapelicious Ooey Gooey gum. Ask anyone!"

"How can we be sure?" asked Phil.

"Because I said so," said Lolly, hugging her bag tight to her chest.

"What else is in that bag?" asked Adam. "More candy?"

"You can't just go accusing me because you don't know who else could have done it," said Lolly. "It's not fair. I was helping with the investigation and everything."

Frank and Joe looked at each other.

"She's right," admitted Frank. "Plus, there's only gum in her bag—and Heather said there were toys and other kinds of candy in the piñata."

"And real detectives have to have a reason to go through people's things—our dad told us," Frank added.

Joe nodded. "It's called 'probably cause.'"

"*Probable* cause," corrected Frank. "And it means we need to leave Lolly alone, unless we have a real reason to believe she stole the candy."

Cissy shrugged. "Lolly *probably* took the candy, *'cause* she loves to eat it so much! She's sugar crazy!"

"But that's also the reason why she could be telling the truth," Frank reasoned. "She loves candy, so it shouldn't be a big surprise that she's carrying a bunch of it around in her bag."

"Okay," said Joe. He faced Lolly—he couldn't help but feel bad for her. "If something else comes up and it looks suspicious for you, though, will you agree to show us everything in your bag?"

Lolly nodded. "I guess."

"Let's go," Adam said to his team. "This is getting boring."

Cissy, Adam, Seth, and Tony stalked off with their Y-shaped sticks. Phil put the stick he'd found before the sword fight into a clue bag. It was time to open the new clue—before Adam's team beat them.

Lolly smiled her thanks at the Hardy boys and offered them, and Phil, a piece of purple gum, which they took and popped in their mouths, competing to see who could blow the biggest bubble.

"Howdy there, kids!" boomed Ranger Bo, coming upon the group. "How's your scavenger hunt going?"

"We're just about to open Clue Number Four," said Phil excitedly.

Ranger Bo patted the pockets of his brown pants, then his jacket pockets, as if he was looking for something. "Clue Number Four?" he asked. "That's my favorite!"

"Really?" asked Phil. "How come?"

"Open it up and find out for yourself!" said Ranger Bo. "I'm off to look for my hat."

With that, Bo walked off, looking under park benches and picnic tables as he went.

"Did anyone else notice his hat was on his head?" asked Phil.

"Me!" chorused Lolly, Frank, and Joe.

"He really is forgetful, isn't he?" said Frank.

The team sat at a wooden picnic table while Joe opened the fourth clue. They leaned in as he read it aloud:

> *"I turn color in fall*
> *but that's not all.*
> *I should have a few holes;*
> *being bug food take its tolls."*

The group thought for a minute.

"I understand the first part," said Frank, running his finger over the grooves in the picnic tabletop. "But not the second."

"What's the first part?" Joe asked.

"Leaves?" said Phil. "Leaves turn colors in the fall."

"Exactly," agreed Frank. "But what's the bug part?"

"Don't bugs eat leaves?" Lolly asked, snapping her purple bubble gum. It was already fading, turning from bright purple to lavender.

Joe nodded. "Yup, they do! And when they eat the leaves . . ."

"They leave holes in the leaf!" said Frank, under-standing.

"So we're looking for a bug-eaten leaf with holes in it for proof?" asked Phil.

"That's right," said Frank. "Where should we start?"

"I think it's time to go into the woods," suggested Lolly, rising from her seat. "There are more leaves there than anywhere else in the park."

The boys followed her lead, all the way to the wooded path. They saw a few different teams on their way. Elisa had just found her Y-shaped stick, and Ellie Freeman's team hadn't even managed to make their mud yet!

But Adam's team was still neck and neck with the Hardys' team.

"I think we should look here," said Lolly, stop-ping in front of a big, leafy elm tree. "This one has a ton of leaves—some of them must have bug holes."

"Good idea," said Frank.

Lolly and Frank focused on the leaves they could reach on the tree, and Phil and Joe knelt down and checked the fallen leaves on the ground.

Frank got on his toes and pulled a leaf off the tree. For the most part, it was smooth and bright green, like the grass. But it had four tiny, pin-size holes in one corner where the edges were browning.

"Got one!" he exclaimed.

But when he turned to look at his team, they were all looking past him, under the tree.

Frank turned to follow their gaze. There, mixed in with the leaves and branches right next to the tree trunk, was a bunch of shredded yellow paper.

"It's from the piñata!" shouted Phil.

Joe picked some shreds up and examined them. He spotted a blur of movement out of the corner of his eye and looked up.

"Look!" Joe said. "Up there!"

Chapter
7

TREE HUGGER

There, standing on a thick, sturdy branch just above
Frank and Joe Hardy's heads, was Heather.

"Ranger Heather?" said Lolly, her mouth drop-
ping open.

Frank couldn't see what Heather was doing, but
he noticed that one of her arms was raised high in
the air, as if she was trying to reach something.

Heather lowered her arm, and when she did, Frank
and Joe saw that she had her phone in her hand.

"Be right down!" She wrapped her hands around one branch, then another, making her way down from the tree.

By the time Heather finally jumped to the ground, she had a leaf in her perfect hair, and pieces of broken tree bark clung to her ranger uniform.

"I was just trying to get better phone service," she told them.

"In the tree?" Phil asked.

Heather nodded. "This park gets, like, no Wi-Fi."

Phil looked confused. "Of course not," he said. "It's a park!"

Joe leaned in to whisper to his brother. "Do you think she could be a suspect?" he asked.

Frank wasn't sure. It looked suspicious that they'd found Heather so close to pieces of the piñata. But what was her motive for stealing it in the first place? Frank leaned down, picked up the shredded yellow paper bits, and stuck them in one of the clue bags for their scavenger hunt items.

"What's that?" Heather asked, pointing at the pieces of piñata in Frank's bag.

"Evidence," explained Joe.

"Of what?" Heather asked. She plucked a tub of lip gloss from her front pocket and smoothed the sticky, shiny goo over her lips.

"We're investigating the case of the missing scavenger hunt prize," Frank said.

Heather's phone chimed like a bell—it was the same sound Mrs. Hardy's phone made whenever she got a text.

Heather tapped her phone a couple of times, made a few swipes across the screen, and then locked it. She placed the phone back in her pocket and looked up at them.

Joe wondered if she'd really been listening to what his brother had said. "Did you see anyone around here looking like they were up to trouble?" he asked Heather.

"I don't think so," she said. "Why?"

"Because," Frank said, holding up the bagged pieces of piñata, "we found the missing piñata pieces right here under this tree."

Heather raised her eyebrows. "I wonder how those got there."

Joe looked at her warily. "We were hoping you could tell us that."

Heather leaned forward, placing her hands on her knees so that she was closer to Joe's height. "Why?" she asked. "Am I a suspect?" She laughed, throwing her head back a little like it was the funniest thing she'd ever heard.

"We're not ruling anyone out," said Frank carefully. He didn't want to single her out the way Adam had with Lolly earlier, but he didn't want to lie, either.

"I think it's time for you kids to get back to your scavenger hunt," Heather said, looking skeptical. "Ranger Bo just texted me—he's gone out to get the new prize, and I'm in charge while he's gone."

"How come he didn't want you to go?" Phil asked, voicing a question that was in Frank's head.

Back at the visitors' cabin, Heather had seemed to really want to go out to get the new prize herself. Ranger Bo had said no pretty quickly—and Frank and Joe wanted to know why.

Heather twirled her hair around a seashell-pink-painted fingertip. She bit her lip, as though she wanted to say something but wasn't sure if she should.

"Ranger Bo is my dad," Heather said finally. "He

doesn't like me to leave the park during work hours, because he's afraid I'll be on my phone the whole time."

Frank and Joe exchanged a look. Did that count as a motive? If Heather was mad at her dad, maybe she'd have sabotaged the scavenger hunt prize. Or . . .

Far off in the distance, Frank heard a bunch of squeals and shouts. The team jogged down the path and searched the path through the trees to see what was going on.

It was Adam's team!

"We're going to win!" Cissy shouted. She turned to Adam, who was holding a clue envelope. "Just one clue left—hurry up and open it!"

Fweeeeeeet!

Just behind Frank and Joe stood Heather, her whistle still in her mouth.

"Twenty minutes left!" she shouted. "Twenty minutes! Finish

up your last clue and meet back in the visitors' cabin in twenty minutes!"

"Oh no!" said Joe, turning to the team. "Adam's team is beating us, and we haven't even solved the mystery yet. What do we do?"

Lolly held up the final clue. "You help us solve the clue, and Phil and I will go find it while you two work out the mystery. Sound like a plan?"

"Let's do it!" said Joe.

Chapter 8

STAY BACK!

When animals travel,
they leave this mark.
Last clue to unravel
in Bayport Bear Park!

"The note at the bottom of the clue says that we have to take a picture of two different examples, instead of putting whatever it is in a plastic bag," said Phil.

Frank tucked the last clue away in his back pocket. This was the hardest clue yet, but he knew that if they worked together, they could solve it.

"Animals travel?" Lolly asked. "What does that mean?"

"Let's think. How do animals travel?" Frank asked.

"Bunnies hop," suggested Lolly.

"And birds fly," Joe said. "But I don't know what that has to do with the clue." He leaned against the maple tree behind him, causing a squirrel nearby to startle and scamper away. As it ran, the squirrel scattered a spray of dirt and crunched through old fallen leaves.

Frank tiptoed toward the leaves the squirrel had upset. "Wait a minute," he said. "Did you guys see that?"

"What?" asked Phil. "The squirrel?"

Frank knelt down and looked closely at the ground. It was faint, but when he pushed aside the leaves and branches, Frank could see where the squirrel had left an imprint of his paw in the dirt. It looked like a mini version of a dog's paw print, but with little lines at the ends where the claws were.

"Look!" Frank said, calling them over.

"Is that from the squirrel?" Joe asked, peering at the print in the dirt.

"When it ran, it left its mark!" Phil exclaimed.

"The answer to the clue is animal tracks," said Joe. "So if we take a picture of the squirrel's paw print, that means we're done!"

"Almost," corrected Lolly. She popped another

piece of Ooey Gooey into her mouth and chewed around her words. "It says we have to take a picture of *two* different animal tracks. We only have one."

Phil took out his phone and snapped a picture of the squirrel print. Then he reminded Frank and Joe that he and Lolly would look for the next set of tracks while the Hardys went to work on solving the scavenger hunt heist.

The group went deeper into the woods, making sure to stick to the trails. Around them, they could hear other groups moving around. Chet Morton and Elisa Locke were bagging their bug-eaten leaf to their right, and Ellie Freeman was just reading the last clue aloud to her team.

Joe didn't see Adam or anyone else from Adam's group, so there was no way to know whether they'd already found their first tracks. He pushed the thought out of his mind. It was time to focus on their case!

"Okay," Frank said. "We have fifteen minutes left to solve this case—let's get cracking!"

"I'll set my timer," said Joe.

Frank could feel his heart pounding. He'd never had to solve a case to a timer before, and with so little to go on!

As they walked, Frank pulled out his trusty notebook and showed his brother what they had so far:

> *Who: Adam? Lolly? Ranger Heather?*
> *What: stolen piñata*
> *When: between 11:30 and 11:40 a.m.*
> *Where: Bear Park visitors' cabin*
> *Why: ????*

"Let's start with Adam," suggested Frank. "Why would he want to steal the prize?"

Joe shrugged. "Adam doesn't *need* a reason to cause trouble," he said. "He just does!"

"True," Frank said, sidestepping a fallen tree branch. "What about . . ." He lowered his voice. "Lolly?"

"I heard that!" Lolly called from ahead, glancing at the Hardys.

Frank felt bad, but Lolly was smiling, which

made him feel a bit better. Joe and Frank walked fast to catch up with Lolly and Phil.

"My motive is simple," Lolly added, surprising the two brothers. "Everyone knows how much I love candy!"

"Um, that's true," said Frank, making a note next to her name.

"What's Heather's motive, then?" asked Joe.

"She could have done it because she was mad at her dad," said Frank, making another note. "Maybe she wanted to get back at him for not letting her be on her phone?"

"You guys might be great detectives," Lolly said, ducking under a low-hanging branch. "But you don't know anything about girls!"

"I think I see something up there," Phil said. He pointed toward where the path broke off in two different directions. He jogged ahead.

"What do you mean, Lolly?" asked Frank.

"Heather was awfully quick to volunteer to run out and get a new prize after we discovered the original one had been stolen," Lolly added.

"You think she could have stolen the prize just for the excuse to leave and get a new one?" Frank asked.

Lolly nodded. "That way, she could be on her phone all she wanted!"

Up ahead, Phil had stopped at the fork in the path and was pulling out his phone.

"Did you find something?" Joe called out, running to look over Phil's shoulder.

"Uh-oh," said Joe, looking down at the tracks in the dirt. "Frank, you better not come any closer!"

"What are you talking about?" said Frank, going right for his brother.

"What are they?" Phil asked Joe.

But it wasn't Joe who answered him.

Frank stared at the tracks in the dirt—rounder, fatter versions of the squirrel tracks they'd seen earlier. But these tracks were about ten times the size of the squirrel's. Where had he seen those before?

That was when he remembered—the documentary! "B-b-b-bear tracks!"

Chapter 9

DON'T FEED THE ANIMALS

"I got the picture—let's get out of here!" yelled Phil.

They all turned to leave, except Frank Hardy.

"Frank, are you crazy?" Joe asked. "You were the one who was so afraid of the bears! Let's go!"

Frank's heart was pounding—but not for the reason it was earlier, when he'd first gotten off the school bus. Not only did he have to solve a case so soon, but he felt like they were super close to figuring it out!

"C'mon, Frank!" Lolly urged, tugging the cuff of his jacket sleeve.

"Can we please get out of here?" Phil asked. "In case you didn't notice, we're about to be bear stew!"

"I don't think we're in any danger," Frank said. He hoped not, anyway. But it didn't stop his heart from pounding, or his hands from shaking.

Frank looked at his brother, who was now looking at the bear tracks. Joe met his eyes and nodded.

"You see what I see, don't you?" Frank asked.

Joe nodded. "The tracks are going the wrong way."

Lolly sighed. "What are you two talking about?" she asked. "And why aren't we moving?"

"The tracks aren't leading deeper into the woods, the way they should be," Frank explained.

"Where are they leading?" Phil asked, looking horror-struck.

"That's what I plan to find out!" Frank said.

With Frank leading the way, the whole team began to follow the bear tracks—very carefully. They walked off the path, through the thicket of trees and over fallen branches and logs. The sun streamed through the treetops, shining its light on the trail like a flashlight.

"We'd better not get lost!" Lolly said. "Ranger Bo said not to go off the path."

"We're not lost," said Joe. "It's kind of hard to see the tracks, though." He pointed up ahead in the distance, to a big maple tree with polished-looking reddish-purple leaves. "I remember that tree! See how the one next to it has a big hole at the center of the trunk? I remember thinking it looked like a mouth, yawning."

"Where did we see that before?" Phil asked, scratching his head.

Suddenly Frank gasped. "It's where we found our first clue—the feather!"

Lolly drew her eyebrows together in thought. "But that tree was behind the—"

"The tracks are leading right to the visitors' cabin!" Joe finished for her.

"No way!" said Phil. His eyes grew wide.

"I don't like this," Lolly said, her voice wobbling.

"Oh no!" Frank said. "We've got to get back there

and make sure our classmates aren't in danger!"

Joe leaned toward his brother and spoke in a low voice, so only Frank could hear. "But aren't you afraid?"

Frank tilted his chin up. "I'm still afraid. But we have to help the others."

Behind the group, a sound echoed through the woods—the sound of a twig snapping, then another.

Someone was gaining on them! Or some*thing* . . .

"Run!" Joe shouted, hooking his brother's elbow with his own.

Now that the noise was behind them, they ran toward the cabin. Even though it wasn't that far, it felt like forever!

Frank and Joe led the pack, vaulting over a fallen tree limb, then ducking beneath a low-hanging canopy of vines and leaves.

"Don't look back!" Frank told his team as footsteps pounded behind them. "It will only slow us down!"

Thud, thud, thud.

Phil gasped for air. "I don't think I can run any-more!"

"Yes, you can!" shouted Lolly. She grabbed his hand and pulled him forward, alongside her.

"I see the cabin up ahead!" said Joe. "Just a little bit farther!"

As they ran they began to see something yellow that had not been there earlier just off the path. At first it looked like it might be a patch of yellow dandelions, or some kind of wildflower blooming in time for spring.

When they were closer, they saw it was ripped-up pieces of paper from the stolen piñata!

"More piñata pieces!" Joe told Frank. "The paper trail is leading back out to the woods!"

There was a low sound coming from behind them—a deep, rumbling roar.

"Was that a growl?" Phil asked as he ran, the fear plain in his voice.

Frank could almost reach out and touch the back doorknob of the visitors' cabin—they were so close!

The rumble sounded once again, this time louder.

Grrrrrr. Grrrrrrr!

"I heard it too!" said Lolly.

"Everyone get inside," Frank said, finally grabbing the doorknob and yanking it open. "Quick!"

"Are you guys okay?" asked Ranger Bo from inside the cabin.

"Shut the door, quick!" Frank told him. "Bear!"

Ranger Bo pulled the door shut once Joe, Frank, Lolly, and Phil were all inside, safe. He peered out the window, the silver in his hair catching a glint in the sunlight.

"Where did you see a bear?" he asked. The usually cheerful look on his face had turned serious.

"We didn't see it," said Joe, "but we heard it!"

On cue, the rumbling started back up outside.

"There it is again!" Frank said.

"That?" Ranger Bo said.

Frank and Joe nodded. To their surprise, Ranger Bo started laughing a big, bearlike belly laugh.

Frank narrowed his eyes. This was no laughing matter!

"I'm sorry, kids," said Ranger Bo. "What you heard isn't a bear."

"It's not?" asked Lolly.

"Then what is it?" Joe asked, crossing his arms.

"See for yourself," Ranger Bo said. He opened the door, and right away, Frank heard the rumbling get louder.

A small machine, about half the size of a car, moved across the grass slowly. There was a man behind the wheel.

"A lawn mower?" Frank asked, embarrassed.

Ranger Bo nodded.

"But something was with us in the woods," argued Lolly. "It was following us!"

"Oh, that?" said a voice in the cabin.

When Frank turned, he saw Adam Ackerman—looking very proud of himself. He smiled. "That was me."

"You chased us?" Frank said angrily. "Why?"

Adam shrugged. "You always think you're better than everyone else. With your stupid mystery club and your dumb notebook. I just wanted to prove that you aren't as brave as you think you are!"

Frank's face burned. He *had* been pretty afraid; Adam was right about that.

"You're wrong," said Lolly, taking a step toward Adam. "Frank is brave."

Frank looked at her, confused. "What do you mean?" he asked. "As soon as we heard those noises in the woods, I ran!"

"Yeah," Lolly said. "But even though you were afraid of the bear, you still followed the tracks to the cabin. You did it to make sure everyone was safe! That's brave."

Ranger Bo stared. "Tracks?" he asked. But no one was paying attention.

Adam sniffed. "Whatever. You still didn't solve your stupid case."

Frank and Joe grinned at each other.

"Do you want to tell him?" Joe asked. "Or should I?"

"I'll get this one," Frank said, pulling his notebook out of his pants pocket and opening it up. "According to my 'stupid notebook,'" he said, "we *did* solve the case."

"Oh yeah?" said Adam, looking doubtful. "Then who did it?"

"No one." Frank smiled. "At least, no one here."

THE HARDY BOYS—and
YOU!

CAN YOU SOLVE THE MYSTERY OF THE MISSING PIÑATA?

Grab a piece of paper and write your answers down.
Or just turn the page to find out.

1. Frank and Joe came up with a list of suspects.
   Can you think of more? List your suspects.

2. How do you think the piñata disappeared
   from the cabin? Using the "proof" the boys
   have so far, write your ideas down!

3. What clues helped you to solve the mystery?
   Write them down!

Chapter

10

THE BEAR TRUTH

"It was . . . a bear!" Frank said.

Ranger Bo chuckled, patting his chest as he did. "You boys are so funny. What a great joke!"

"You *are* kidding, aren't you?" asked Phil.

Frank shook his head. "When we were looking for animal tracks, we found bear tracks. But they were going *toward* the cabin!"

"And once we got closer to the cabin," Joe said,

"we found shredded bits of the piñata all over the ground, leading back out to the woods."

"Just like the pieces we found out by the tree when we found Heather trying to get better phone service," Frank added.

Ranger Bo frowned. "She is supposed to be helping out—she is on that phone way too much."

Proof! Frank thought, remembering what his dad had told him earlier that morning. He was glad they hadn't gone around accusing all the wrong people of stealing, now that he knew who had really done it. He knew his dad would be proud of him and Joe.

Ranger Bo's mouth dropped open. "But— that's—how—?"

"You said yourself not to feed the animals, right?" said Frank.

"Well, yes," he said.

Frank pointed to the back door. "When we asked Lolly if she'd seen anyone in the cabin earlier—just before the piñata went missing—she said that she was here alone."

"She also said that the back door was open," added Joe.

Ranger Bo put his head in his hands. "Oh no!" he said.

"What's wrong?" asked Lolly.

"I left the door open!" He shook his head. "I can't believe I did that! I'm just so forgetful!"

Frank and Joe remembered earlier in the day, when Ranger Bo had walked away looking for his hat—and it had been right on his head!

"The bear must have been attracted to the candy!" Ranger Bo said. "You boys are right; the bear stole your prize candy!"

"The bear ate all that candy," Lolly said, looking impressed.

"And the toys, too, probably," added Phil.

Just then Heather walked through the front door of the cabin. And in her arms was a great big chocolate-brown piñata—in the shape of a bear!

"I finished filling it with the new candy and toys, Dad," she announced, setting it on the table. "Do we have a winner yet?"

The other teams had been trickling in slowly while Frank and Joe were talking to Ranger Bo. Now they all ran over to examine the new scavenger hunt prize.

Ranger Bo gathered everyone in a circle. He asked them all to pull out their bags of collected clues.

Ellie Freeman's team had found all but the last set of tracks, and Elisa's team had collected every single item, but their Y-shaped twig had broken during the hunt, so it wasn't Y-shaped anymore.

Adam's team and Frank and Joe's team had both collected all the items from the clues, but only one of them had taken pictures of two sets of animal tracks. Squirrel *and* bear tracks!

Ranger Bo beamed down at Frank and Joe Hardy. "Congratulations, kids! It looks like your team gets the piñata!"

Lolly was smiling so wide, it looked like her face would crack! And Phil and Frank were already talking about which toys they hoped would be inside.

Once Heather had hung the piñata up in the middle of the room, she handed Frank a plastic baseball bat. "You think you can break it open?" she asked him.

Frank looked at his team. "Does anyone else want to take the first swing?" he asked.

"You should do it," Lolly said. "You solved the mystery, *and* you were brave."

Frank tightened his grip on the baseball bat while Heather blindfolded him.

Joe and Phil spun Frank in a circle—once, twice, three times.

"Are you ready?" Ranger Bo asked.

"I think so," said Frank.

He tried to retrace his steps to where he thought the piñata was. Then he swung the bat!

On his first try, and his second, the bat didn't even hit the piñata. But on the third try, he heard it connect with a soft thunk.

The group cheered behind him.

Next, Phil and Joe both got a turn. Phil didn't even hit the piñata once, but Joe hit it twice! Still, it hadn't broken open.

It was Lolly's turn.

Once she was blindfolded and spun around three times, she gripped the bat and smiled. Then she took four small steps and swung the bat as hard as she could.

She felt the bat connect to the piñata and, all at once, heard the rush of toys and candy spilling out of it, onto the floor!

• • •

Frank and Joe Hardy were surrounded by a mountain of toys and prize candy.

They were sitting in the secret tree house that their dad had built for them in the Hardys' backyard. Joining them were Phil and the latest member of their mystery-solving club—Lolly Sugarman.

"Ughhhh," Joe groaned. "If I eat one more piece of candy, I'm going to puke!"

Lolly popped a strawberry SugarPop lollipop into her mouth and shook her head. "You shouldn't have tried to eat as much as me," she told him, patting his shoulder. "It takes practice to eat as much as I do— at least, that's what my mom tells me."

Phil and Frank were working together on a cube-shaped puzzle with lots of colors.

"I can't move," Joe complained, slumping in his chair.

Frank laughed. "But everything was deeee-licious!"

"Looks like the Hardy boys have solved another mystery," said Phil.

"I'm proud of you, Frank," said Joe. "Not only did we solve the case today, but you faced a really big fear!"

"And lived to tell the tale." Lolly grinned through her lollipop.

"*You* weren't afraid?" Frank asked Joe. "Not even once?"

"Nope!" Joe placed his hands behind his head. "I guess I'm just not ever afraid."

Frank paused, turning to look out the window of the tree house. "Did you guys hear that?"

"What?" Joe asked, sitting up.

"That growling," said Frank. "*Shhhh* . . . I think it's a . . . BEAR ATTACK!" He turned toward his brother and ran at him with his hands up in the air like claws.

"Ahhhh!" Joe screamed.

Frank, Lolly, and Phil doubled over, laughing.

"Our hero," said Frank. "Nothing can scare him!"

"Except my own brother," Joe admitted, joining in the laughter. "And maybe Aunt Gertrude when she tells me to clean my room."

"I think I could get used to being a part of this club," Lolly said, grinning.

Another case solved!

P7-DYO-406

Pup and Hound Lost and Found

For Hollie, my family's puppy love — S.H.

For the Roske "pups" — L.H.

 Kids Can Read is a registered trademark of Kids Can Press Ltd.

Text © 2006 Susan Hood
Illustrations © 2006 Linda Hendry

Kids Can Press acknowledges the financial support of the Government
of Ontario, through the Ontario Media Development Corporation's
Ontario Book Initiative; the Ontario Arts Council; the Canada Council
for the Arts; and the Government of Canada, through the BPIDP, for
our publishing activity.

Published in Canada by
Kids Can Press Ltd.
29 Birch Avenue
Toronto, ON M4V 1E2

Published in the U.S. by
Kids Can Press Ltd.
2250 Military Road
Tonawanda, NY 14150

www.kidscanpress.com

The artwork in this book was rendered in pencil crayon on a sienna
colored pastel paper.
The text is set in Bookman.

Series editor: Tara Walker
Edited by Yvette Ghione
Printed and bound in China

The hardcover edition of this book is smyth sewn casebound.

CM 06 0 9 8 7 6 5 4 3 2 1
CM PA 06 0 9 8 7 6 5 4 3 2 1

Library and Archives Canada Cataloguing in Publication

Hood, Susan
        Pup and hound lost and found / written by Susan Hood ;
illustrated by Linda Hendry.
(Kids Can read) 3299 5077/06
ISBN-13: 978-1-55337-806-8 (bound) ISBN-10: 1-55337-806-7 (bound)
ISBN-13: 978-1-55337-807-5 (pbk.) ISBN-10: 1-55337-807-5 (pbk.)

I. Hendry, Linda II. Title. III. Series: Kids Can read (Toronto, Ont.)

PZ7.H758Pupl 2006   j813'.54   C2005-903893-4

Kids Can Press is a *CORUS*™ Entertainment company

Pup and Hound
Lost and Found

Written by Susan Hood

Illustrated by Linda Hendry

Kids Can Press

What was that —

that *vroom, vroom* sound?

Look, Pup!

The truck is going to town!

So Pup and Hound

leaped from their chair.

They hitched a ride ...

... to the county fair!

Flags and banners flapped

in the sky.

"Yip, yap!" barked Pup

as a blimp flew by.

Hound sniffed the air.

He sniffed something dandy —

hot dogs and pretzels

and — oooh! — cotton candy!

Pushing their way

through people's knees,

Hound hurried Pup

past a circus of fleas.

They stopped for a snack.

They begged for a treat.

A little girl gave them

all they could eat.

The loudspeaker blared,
"Friends, take your places!
It's time to begin
the Poky Pig Races!"

Ten squealing piglets raced
around the track.
But Pup wandered off
when Hound turned his back.

Hound watched the piglets

race on and on.

When he turned around —

oh, dear! — Pup was gone!

"Woof!" There he was

behind the hay bale!

No, it was just a pony's tail.

Wait! Over there!

Were those Pup's paws?

No! It was a cat

with very sharp claws!

Was that little Pup?

Look! Right up there!

No, it was just a teddy bear.

Hound sniffed the ground.

Where would Pup go?

Would the man on stilts

or the juggler know?

Hound tracked Pup's trail

from place to place.

He dodged little kids

in a three-legged race.

He looked in each barn.

He looked in each stall.

He asked all the cows.

No Pup at all!

Hound looked high.

And Hound looked low.

Where was that Pup?

Where did he go?

Wait! What was that?

Hound heard people clapping!

He picked up Pup's scent,

then heard his friend yapping.

Hound raced past the barns,

past some sheep and a goose ...

... to find Pup in charge
of the kissing booth!

$1.0